It could not have been done without:

Stephan Henrich,
Ezio Blasetti,
Gwyllim Jahn,
Danielle Willems,
Vongsawat Wongkijjalerd,
Myrtille Fakhreddine,
Daniela Mitterberger,
Katrin Hochschuh,
Tiziano Derme,
Agatha Partyka,
Chantale,
...
and many others

(see full credits at the end of the book)

-
--

We are very tired already

0.0 And by annihilating the body humans pretended to become apolitical
0.1 Places of physical resistance were losing importance What mattered always was the mind and its amusement #entertainment #momentaryescapes #bodyindenial
(did physical love equal freedom in 1984?)
0.2 We were now to reveal entrapments

...

1.0 This is a call for rituals
For screams and procedures
Control, outlets
1.1 Remember
When man's life was organized through a succession of rituals
Where you would find your place as an individual
Protocoled duties soaked with meaning to allow for freedom within
Also, the psycho-physical territory where you could play, trespass reason's limits
One would allow for madness and meet what madness could give
1.2 Allow for gestures, crafted movements, repetition, exhaustion

Architecture is the crime scene

2.0 Hell and Paradise are not places but paths, journeys for remembrance, placeholders for memorising virtues and vices, instructions and signals to follow or avoid #thejourneyandnotthedestination
2.1 We always meant to start with language
The format is content, the path destination, the place a device, a Pilgrim's progress
Making ways to reach mind-places, images, ideas, and their associations
2.2 Disposable, re-usable, able to host even contradictory discourses #placesasdatabases
Here we misplace #misplacement
3.0 However, we need to touch, to confront matter
We need the senses; hearing, caressing, little physical hurts
... Do we produce or do we filter senses?

3.1 The material will lead you somewhere you wouldn't expect at first
3.2 We have had enough of forms and formulas
We are to corrupt the mind, almost a technological device, with sensual friction and norm transgression
3.3 My idols are hackers; technological transgression directly problematic, hence political

Buildings like weapons depending on and servile to technology and its display

4.0 We should always quote: Soul is only a word for something about the body (Nietzsche)
4.1 We should remember: Body and spirit are not inscribed in a precise private space but in a game of spaces, forces, enigmas, and mysteries between man and his dead ancestors — this would include animals —
The individual is the ephemeral reunion of elements of diverse origins, of which some pre-existed its birth and will survive its death in different combinations defining other individualities
4.2 In some ancient societies there is a continuity in the interpretation of the episodes of dreaming and waking: the body when awaking feels all the tiredness of the travel made by its double, as the newborn body wears the mark of the ancestral elements which are reincarnating in him
The body does not have strict limits, neither inside nor outside, it is continuous
Becoming … #transtransfertransfixedandintrance

~~If one allows for~~ what ~~one calls madness~~ more freedom is welcomed

5.0 Man needs blur
Accidents
Solitudes
We demand permission to be sad, desperate, failures; there should be places for rituals: blood-streaked, oozing, diseased
Places where you can finally feel disgusted
5.1 Meanwhile buildings nowadays take good care of making you dependent; and they accomplish this easily
Poster hangers; buildings as ad displays
Desire of meat, of flesh, of skin and sex — when museums are malls, what else could you build — that you will not

obtain, so you can buy something instead, enslaving you to the point there is no way to realize it any longer #perpetualpromiseofanearingsatisfaction

You have enough names for disorders, not enough places

6.0 Mindscapes
6.1 Is there more to a shelter than to protect the body? The body and its double, the spirit and its double as well
6.2 Perception is never neutral; it is infested with our own fears and desires; and so are the places we inhabit The world we inhabit, first our pathologies
6.3 What about rebirth, coming out, weaning, phases of transformation, mediation, an attempt of dialogue, of communication … a rite of passage

Make it make it don't fake it — fake it 'till you feel it

7.0 Follies #psychoarchitecture
The celebration of one's pathologies, phobias, anxieties, neurosis, psychosis … to allow for madness to be lived, to push a logic …
This logic has to become uncomfortable
7.1 Small scale is a way to build it
7.2 Be beyond narration (depart from Ballard's Vermillion Sands, from the absurd mindscapes of Borges)
7.3 In the becoming, without being … the shelter is a device always in operation, a medium, a manifestation of the mind perhaps … perhaps not much else
An exo-psyche, a space of negotiation between the self with its pathologies, its fears and the outside, the other
If the main subject goes, the shelter goes
But all are fleeing … none of the characters truly belongs here, in that sequence
It is a stolen piece of time … a fragment of place, a sketch of identity, a glimpse into a plausible story
7.4 We barely ask for permission
We extract substances, transform, propose, leave behind
7.5 It persists after we depart; turns problematic
Soon the embodiment of a conflict

Overexploited over-solicited bodies

8.0 Metaphors and/or #mythomaniaS
It seems very literal, dangerously symbolic
Metaphors as vehicles, #mythomaniaS as mind-places
8.1 Bio-eco-consumer and/or mechanical-animal
Our body-cyborg stimulated, electrified, chemically controlled
(*kubernêsis* is the 'action of manoeuvring a ship')
8.2 The mind-machine-making-myths
Trans — transfer — transfixed & in trance, we link it via real-time technologies to reach the territories of fear, when the body becomes tense, animal, endangered

Warp Stabilize — Gamma Correct — Export

9.0 To the solitudes in the network, to each ghost in each shell
Permu(ta)ted bodies, not quite digital, at least mediated, each lost in its own way
9.1 We are children of screens, advertisements and film, our world mediated from birth till death
Do we believe: now everything is cinema
9.2 Millennials, born once the world was already over, made in the network, the enigmatically blank generation, looking at heroic figures of the isolated past, while drooling over perpetual fun and superficial connections, the LIKE generation, my generation, Gen N-E-Y … born within images, slave to the guardian of sleep … generation of happily, voluntarily servile, comfortably numb consumers, while cultural forms get smoother and smoother, narrower and narrower

·

Table of Contents:

« mythomaniaS »
Small apparatuses(1)

The reasons behind this work are unknown to me, but the path it is taking, both demonstrative and absurd, makes this journey, the vector-ization of the emer-gences coming from non-formulated hy-potheses, the only reason possibly able to validate them.

There is no plausible psychological explanation, nor a causal connection between the Object and the Situation. These two are satisfied by their unsta-ble equilibrium, between 'the space' (not to be understood in the Modern sense) and the biological body. They share a psyche, non-dissociable from a state of dependency, of correlation, which cannot be described as a domina-tion system, but as belonging, co-be-longing.

The couple's space-body isn't dedi-cated to a projection, of one onto the other, but instead proceeds by co-ex-tensions, co-existences … in a fold of Artaud. The crime scene is crossed by intimacies-extimacies(2), and the ar-chitecture snakes in and through their flux and reflux.

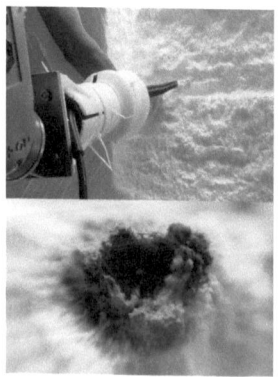

The shelter is no longer dedicated to insularity, a sort of bunker at the service of a vague attempt at the safety of the biological body … it is itself coming from its biologies and allows via its apparatus the certain-ty of transactions, of raw materials and subjectivation … a small osmotic machine, symbiotic and psychic … the

places, the bodies and the misunder-
standings vibrate through their reciprocity … their catatonic stutterings.

We are pulled and pushed in a contradictory mode of exchanges, consub-
stantial to the planet's equilibri-
um-disequilibrium … where we cannot
romanticize the lost natures, the
idealized Holocene, condemned now to
evolve in the Anthropocene, in a thermodynamic flux, unstable and improb-
able … in additive-subtractive mode
… where we are definitively shaping
the planet with our substances, be it
physical, physiological, psychological, (…), where even our psyche has to
be counted in the balance(3).

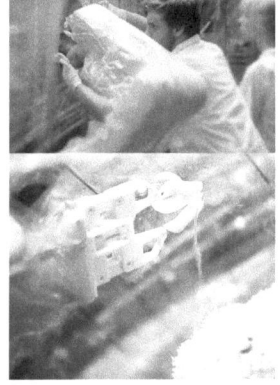

The natures of this Anthropocene are
a source of feedback-backlash vibrations, for a kind of eco-machin-
ist-masochism, in the double paradox
of Labov, both observed and observing
… object and subject, actor and spec-
tator … vector of its "mise en abyme"
…

In positive entropy, no reverse is
possible …

… Psychotic machines, psychotic apparatuses and fragments … Bodies in
verse, bodies-becoming … are meeting
in the stories of their symptoms …
plausible. The "forbidden" is rein-
troduced as a possible, and, what was
rejected or considered as an improper
ingredient within our computer graph-
ic idealization of the world is coming
back like George Bataille's substances … in a repulsive "curiouser and

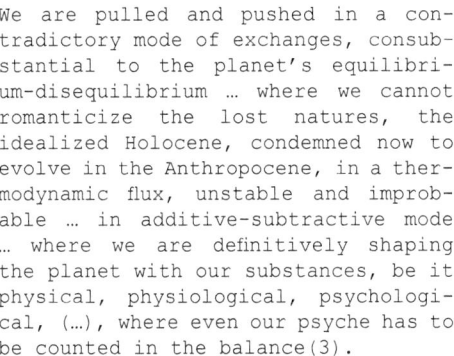

curiouser" affinity, in the pursuit of the notion of risk of Ulrich Beck(4) …

The human being is no longer considered as a bio-eco-consumer but is drifting into a psycho-computing-animal which defi(n)es its situation and condition of living simultaneously with the architecture's emergences, as a co-dependency, a co-relationship … for a Siamese twin alienation. Para-psychoses, projections of the mind, delusions and singularities seem more relevant: Lines of Subjectivities vs Functionalism, Bodies vs Body, Substances vs Shape, Scenario vs Concept … 'Pataphysics(5) vs pseudo-Scientific Positivism … Vanitas(6) vs Naivism …

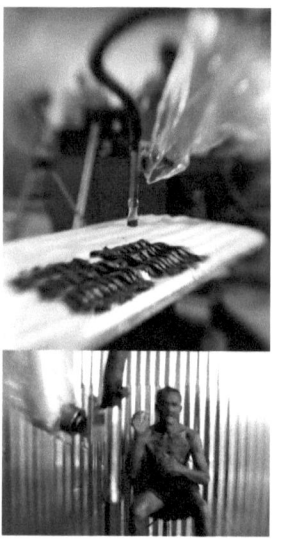

Environments and paranoia as symptoms of an inner condition, in a constant exchange between narrative and emergence, in a stuttering process: a storytelling manifested in the creation of a fiction which uses a fragment as a by-product and where a material structure with its physical characteristics takes shape and instructs the story. Each scenario is a condition of solitude in relation to a "symptomatic symptom" structure, where the fragment is the very "raison d'être" of his/her emotions: the true story of an old Indian book collector exiled from his community on the suspicion of atheism, who finds refuge in a tear-collecting shelter, made of stones and lachrymatories (" … Would Have Been My Last Complaint"); a scientist captured in Anthropocene entropy, condemned to accept metempsychosis exchanges, according to the first principle of thermodynamic

law ("Although (in) hapnea"); a mon-
ster-boy endomorph constantly overfed, protected in a claustrophilic an-
tidote-jacket from the love excess of
his incestuous mother ("(beau)stros-
ity"); the suspended time of Ariadne
floating between two periods, two macho
spirals, testosteroned Theseus and
alcoholic Dionysus ("Terra Insola");
the feral child, innocent, naïve, and
obscene, in the deep jungle, auscul-
tated by scientism and voyeurism ("the
Offspring"); the "difference and repetition" of an affective alienation
become caged food in the pursuit of
Gilles Deleuze ("∑days") ; a post culture spasm … in a mud-dirt-turd where
substances (human psyche and rejec-
tions) meet in their various states of
chemical transformation ("concrete(I)
land"), …

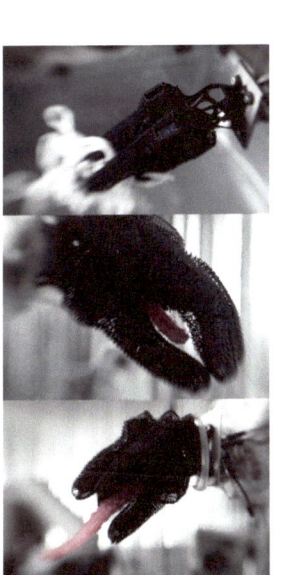

… producing a shelter which produces
a movie and the movie at the origin of
a shelter … as a Siamese twin inter-
laced production, between narration
and topology, able to cross fabrication expertise and human pathologies
to create the condition of a passage,
for a navigation between allusive re-
alism and speculative fiction … inter-
twined, interlocked as a storytelling
developing two collateral effects,
two artifacts: one by the potential
to develop a fiction using an emerg-
ing structure as a by-product, and
the other on the tangible and tactile
world by shaping an emergence which
will "construct" the "raison d'être"
of the story. The relationship, the
permanent flux between the architecture becoming a Prop of another production, in another discipline, and

its own real and fictional footprint
(un)resisting its own erosion, produces an indistinguishable transitory
and transactional process of a Siamese
dialogue … where the two are slipping
in an osmotic, a symbiotic stuttering
… (schizoid protocols within misci-
bility and autonomy …), at the base
of the birth of some twinned fictional
identities … Through the mythomania of
each situation, of each character …
transforming environments with their
para-psyches, confusing Plato's grotto, trajectories, lines of fiction and
physicality. The architecture fragments are becoming the cartography of
their mind from where they can accept the shifting, the drifting … as
a receptacle of their paranoia, but
simultaneously as a vector, a shelter of their emotions. Reprogramming
architecture with psychism … fear and
emotions, relationship aesthetic and
exquisite corpses / placed into the
abyss … to share this schizoid goal …
storytelling and fabrication, but also
to create a laboratory, able to provide the conditions for using and manipulating Sciences and Fictions(7).

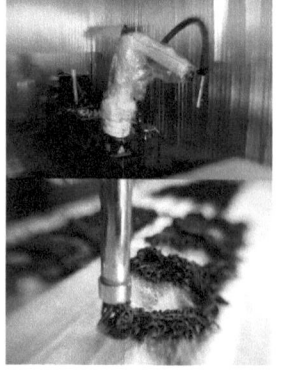

On the side, experiences are under-
taken in Bangkok, through a fab-lab,
M4, including a 6-axes robot, multi-
ples nozzles, a Real Sensor Interface
… a unit of fabrication as an architecture "agenda," confronted with
different biotopes and feedback … in
a permanent challenge to articulate
the contingencies of logic between the
instruments-tooling … as computation,
as robotic, as "de-expertise" of the
design process … with … at the opposite … the discovery of the potential

of a masochism adaptation, for a kind
of "Situationist" claim or debt … in
a strategy-tragedy of correlations …
of co-dependencies … for prototyping
discourses and substances, material
and immaterial(8) …

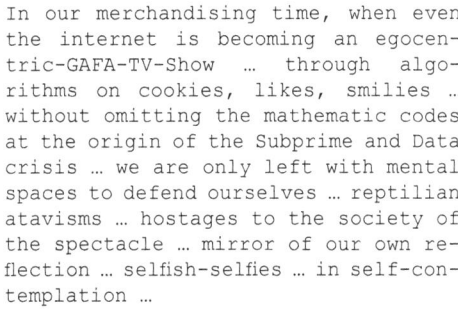

In our merchandising time, when even
the internet is becoming an egocen-
tric-GAFA-TV-Show … through algorithms on cookies, likes, smilies …
without omitting the mathematic codes
at the origin of the Subprime and Data
crisis … we are only left with mental
spaces to defend ourselves … reptilian
atavisms … hostages to the society of
the spectacle … mirror of our own re-
flection … selfish-selfies … in self-con-
templation …

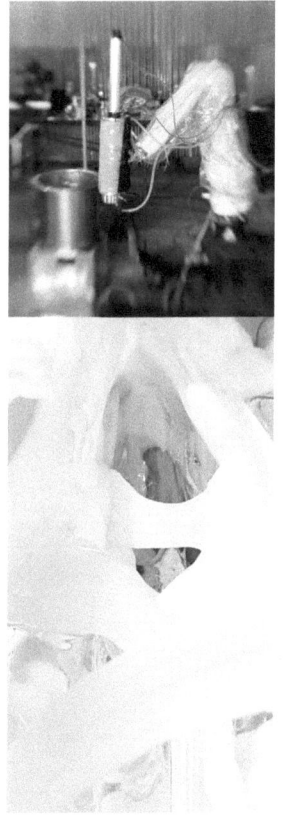

What else could we do than to oppose
this system's obscenity, the obscen-
ity(9) of our pathologies … generated by this very system, affected by
an impossibility to the world, facing
these multiple disorders … to say, to
make-say and make-know … that we as
well are pathogen elements … of this
very disorder, but in a critical mode,
activist, solitary … to produce with
this repulsion … this rejection . in a
metabolised loop … constitutive of the
obscene chain … of these little tales.

Yes, we are only left with obscenity
in order to say, to make, to make-say
and make-know.

This is what we offer here … our pathologies as paranoid-criticism … the
obscenity is not so much the subject
than the voyeurism apparatus which
forces us to look at it, frontally …

In front of the miserabilism of cre-
tinous niches with their hypocritical
formulas(10), we have to re-evaluate
what we used to call "Design"(11) as a
process of synaesthesia, of knowledge
… crossing the multiple conflicts and
embarrassing waste of ideology, criminal positivism, voluntary ignorance,
per formative cynicism … To secrete
from its ambiguity, ambivalence … even
nonsense … absurdity …

… Where some words are definitively
"suspect" relative to daily routines
/ Expertise, Accuracy, Performance,
Optimization, Communication, Futuris-
tic, Future, Innovation, Speculation,
Improvement, Absolute, Truth, Paramet-
ric, Post-Human, Positivism … as the
Grail "onanism" and at the opposite,
other words are vehicles for some kind
of legitimacy … innocently injected
into the daily routine / dirty, filthy,
X-rated, explicit, lewd, rude, vulgar,
coarse, crude, offensive, immoral,
improper, impure, off-color, degener-
ate, depraved, debauched, lubricious,
indecent, smutty, salacious, carnal, lascivious, licentious, bawdy,
and Nostalgia, Melancholia, Metaphor,
but also scatological, profane, porn,
skin, vile, foul, atrocious, outra-
geous, heinous, odious, abhorrent,
abominable, disgusting, hideous, offensive, objectionable, repulsive,
revolting, repellent, loathsome, nau-
seating, sickening, awful, dreadful,
terrible, frightful and repugnant …

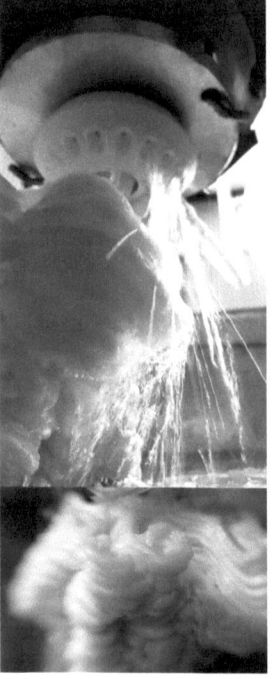

Footnotes

*(1) Referring to Michel Foucault ("un en-
semble hétérogènes d'éléments qui com-
bine des discours et des institutions, des
savoirs et des savoir-faire, du dit et du
non-dit, et qui oriente les attitudes et
les esprits"). This notion has been re-de-
veloped by Giorgio Agamben ... ("J'appelle
dispositif tout ce qui a, d'une manière
ou d'une autre, la capacité de capturer,
d'orienter, de déterminer, d'intercepter,
de modeler, de contrôler, et d'assurer les
gestes, les conduites, les opinions et les
discours des êtres vivants"). Foucault was
developing apparatuses through a strate-
gy of knowledge facing the 'power' (both
strength and political power), including
the reciprocity ... simultaneously co-deter-
mined by their relationship and dependences
(in "The History of Madness") ... Agamben in
"What is an Apparatus?" extended this notion to the electronics, language, tooling
... where the subject is trapped not only
by "institutions, asylum, academia" (from
Foucault's definition), but also by himself
through the objects surrounding him ... It is
the unrevealed intention of these mythomaniaS case studies, through our "Vanities,"
to restore apparatuses in common uses ... to
push their over-coding in visible spectrums
(Deleuze and Guattari use the concept of
over-coding to describe the process whereby
singular human actions are integrated into
dominant social structures ...).*

*(2) The term extimacy (extimité), coined by
Lacan from the term "intimacy" (intimité),
is not the contrary of intimacy. Extimacy
says that the intimate is Other — like a
foreign body, a parasite.*

*(3) As Teillard de Chardin already foresaw
it, the end of the Holocene is not so much
to be attributed to the industrial revolu-
tion but to human thoughts which underpin
it ... the Noosphere, this manufactured evo-
lutionist planetary period, is to be dated
from the Enlightened Century, pre-positiv-
ist scientific operation, which by wanting
to assail guilty obscurantisms, gave birth*

to a proto-capitalist monster (authority of knowledge and discourses). How to judge the City's mathematical algorithms (subprime mortgage crisis & collateralized debt obligations) as well as those of the GAFA (cookies Google-Amazon-Facebook-Apple) as so many systems of influence over the equilibriums of this Anthropocene (remember that Mark Zuckerberg was Awarded the CIA Surveillance Medal as the main Contribution to Monitoring Americans than all other sources combined, and cheaper, too). The re-Terraforming is coming from immaterial, intellectual, scientific and psychic mechanisms.

(4) Ulrich Beck (May 15, 1944 – January 1, 2015) was a German sociologist. His work focused on questions of uncontrollability, ignorance and uncertainty in the modern age, and he coined the terms "risk society" and "second modernity".

(5) 'Pataphysics / (with a prefix apostrophe): the science of imaginary solutions, from Alfred Jarry. The word was first used in 'play Guignol' on April 28 1893. It's a kind of pun, pas ta physique ("not your physics"), and pâte à physique ("physics pastry dough"). The "Collège de 'Pataphysique" was created in 1948 with official members Raymond Queneau, Marcel Duchamp, Chico and Harpo Marx, Man Ray, Eugene Ionesco and unofficial members Jean Genet, John Cage ... We could make some analogy and link between 'Pataphysics and Absurdism, as the two faces of the same coin, the farce on one side, the tragedy on the other.

(6) Vanitas is a type of symbolic work of art especially associated with Eros and Thanatos, extremely morbid and explicit, reflecting an increased obsession with decay also seen in the Danse Macabre.

(7) "Science+fiction" can be defined as that branch of literature which deals with the reaction of human beings to changes in science and technology": from Isaac Asimov, "How Easy to See the Future!", Natural History, #197, 1975.

(8) As the factual pursuit of the LOG#25, edited by Francois Roche in N.York about 'Reclaim Resi[lience]stance' … http://www. new-territories.com/blog/?p=757.

(9) … Bataille in ambush, but also Baudelaire, as a proto-Parnassian, in his battle against Hugolian conventions (Victor Hugo and his compassions for the salon, the boudoir and power), Joyce and his sinthomes, his Guyotat and borborygmi, Artaud and his Catatonias … and Houellebecq … contemporary Pornographic Pictura Negras …

(10) … Being not so digital-romantic, not so computation addict, not so eco-masturbator, not socio-moralist … but just architects, snaking in the crack of abuse, idolatry, idiocracy, propaganda, self-complaisance, bio-hoax, social network lure, etc., could we find a crack between the techno-fetishism (post-Palo Alto symptom in the main Anglo-Saxon schools — for neo-liberalism propaganda and tooling-idiocracy), and at the other end, the techno-regression (mainly in all European schools — Social Kreisel toy for noisy moralism, visible as a parade, a disgusting spectacle at the "common ground" Biennale)? Choosing one of these chapels is so comfortable and self-complaisant … there are many benefices to be blind to or to falsify consciousness and knowledge. But both sides are just the two faces of the same coin … a Janus-like reciprocity of personal interest …! At the opposite, techno-sciences should no longer be an Object, but a Subject we have to re-appropriate and corrupt, with "democratic anthropo-technic" strategies (not in an Art-Deco bio-design show for dummies) …

(11) Design, at the opposite of its English definition, which lost its validity this last 20 years to be exclusively determined by performance and rules, "Design is the creation of a plan or convention for the construction of an object or a system," to quote US Wikipedia … In the French definition, it includes the notion of "dessin/ dessein".

name:	(beau)strosity
year:	2013
location:	Chakkrawat, Bangkok, Thailand
pathology:	claustrophilic bulimia nervosa
prop:	200 laser-cut resin paper components \\ 3 weeks
duration:	04:52
pitch:	baby blues endlessness | fibroid uterine | me in motherland

/ affected-affective zone / bitter-sweet flirt with the obscene / spikulating formation / nobody thought it was forbidden said dolto / confined in the family bond / overfed / extension of her domain from his  flesh / fetus-like fat // sweating amniotic fluid / psycho- umbilical affect / for tacitly t r a n s f i g u r e d m i s p l a c e d emotions / nurture i n g u r g i t a t i o n / fish-bones and surplus / stacking / its growth entangled with mine / the first cavity / porous to her voice and noises /

Françoise Dolto was a pedo-psychiatry specialist. She revolutionized the field of psycho-therapeutic work with the mother-baby dyad, relative to the means of communication used by children with social disabilities.

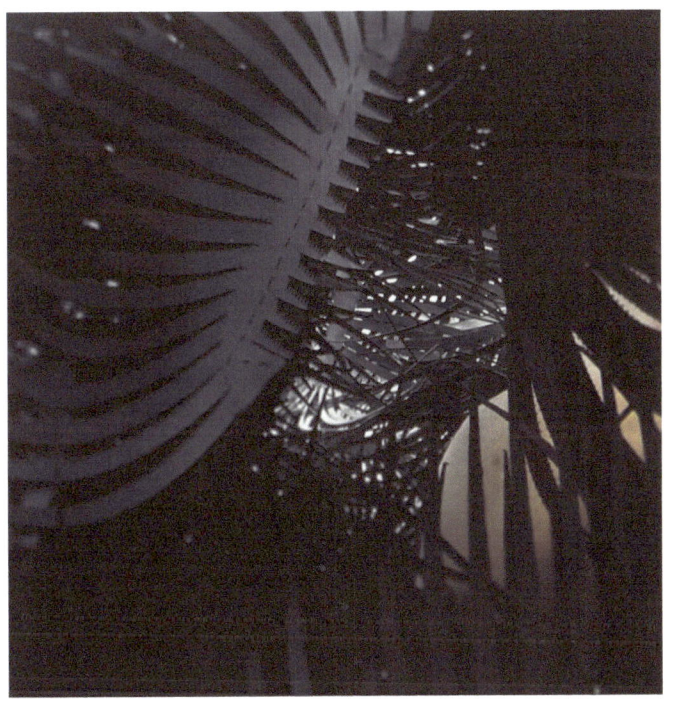

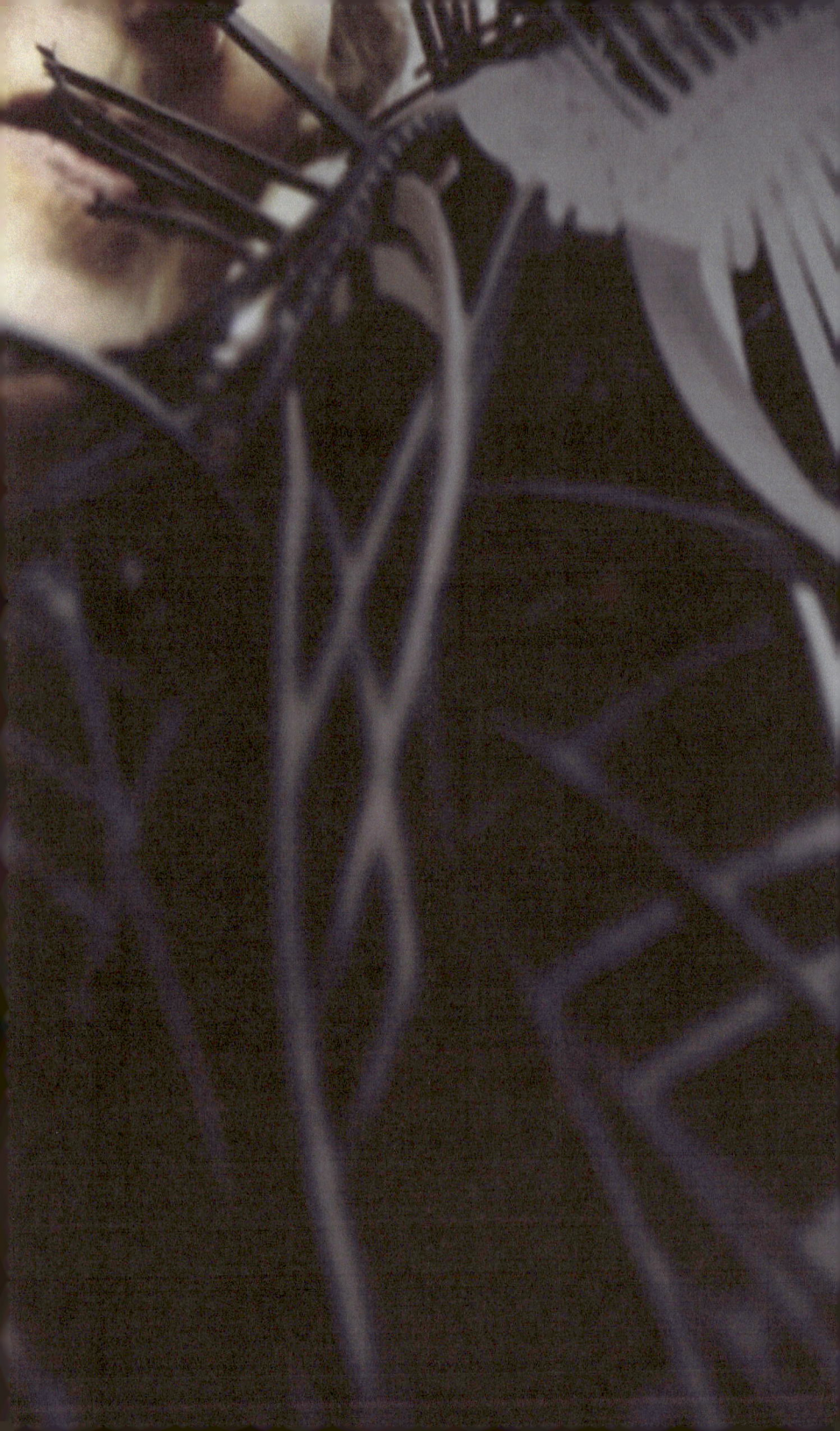

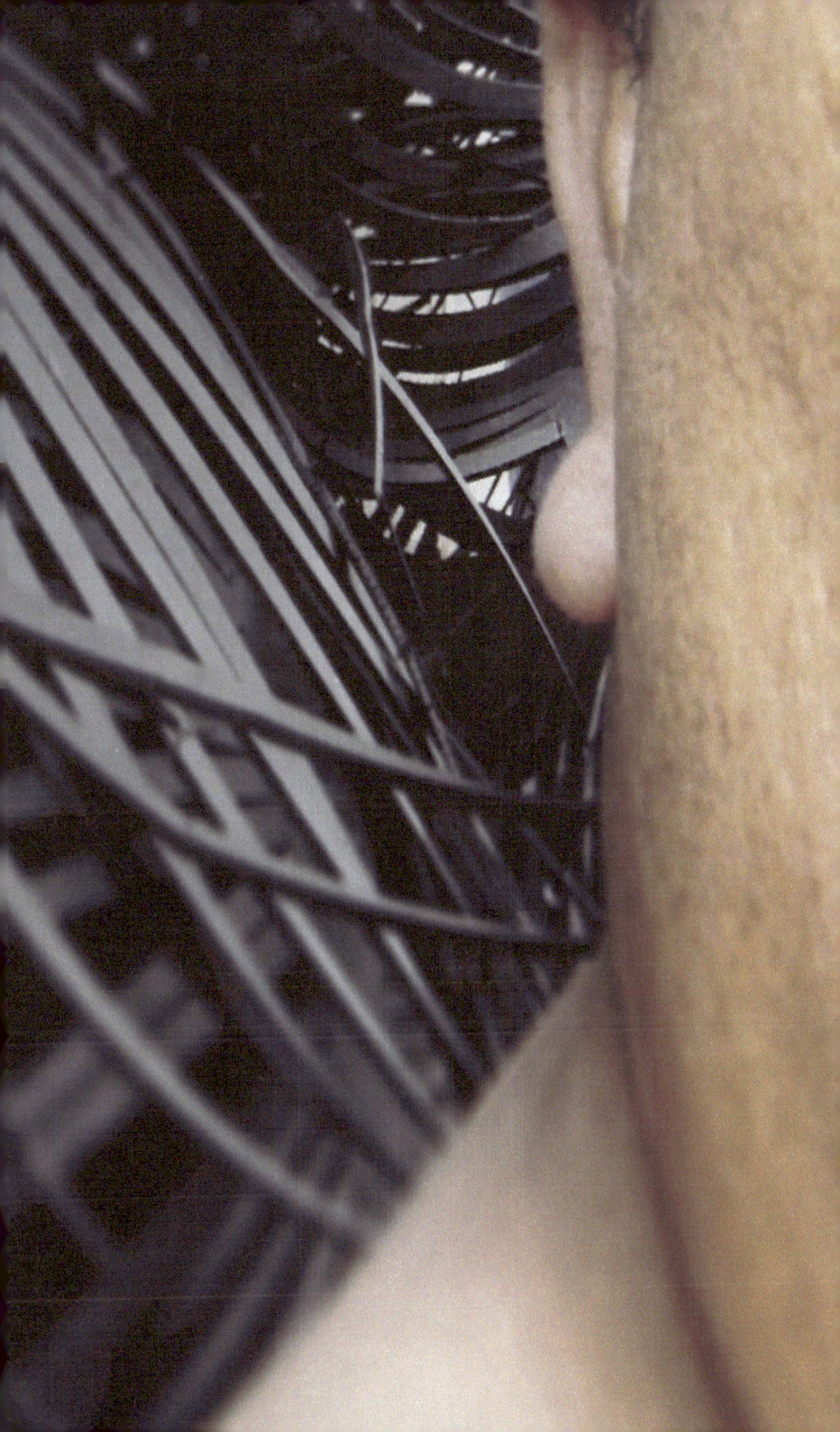

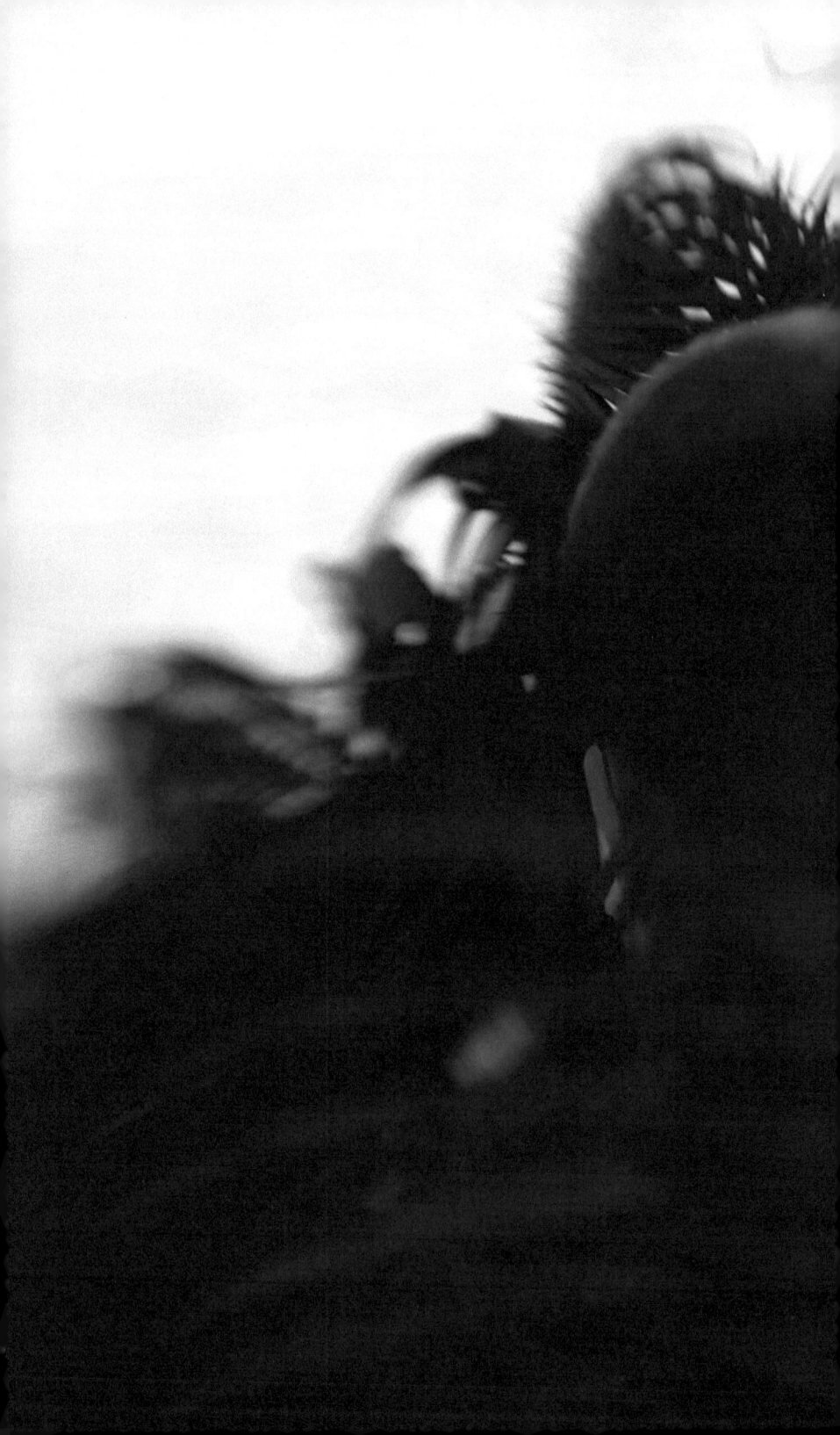

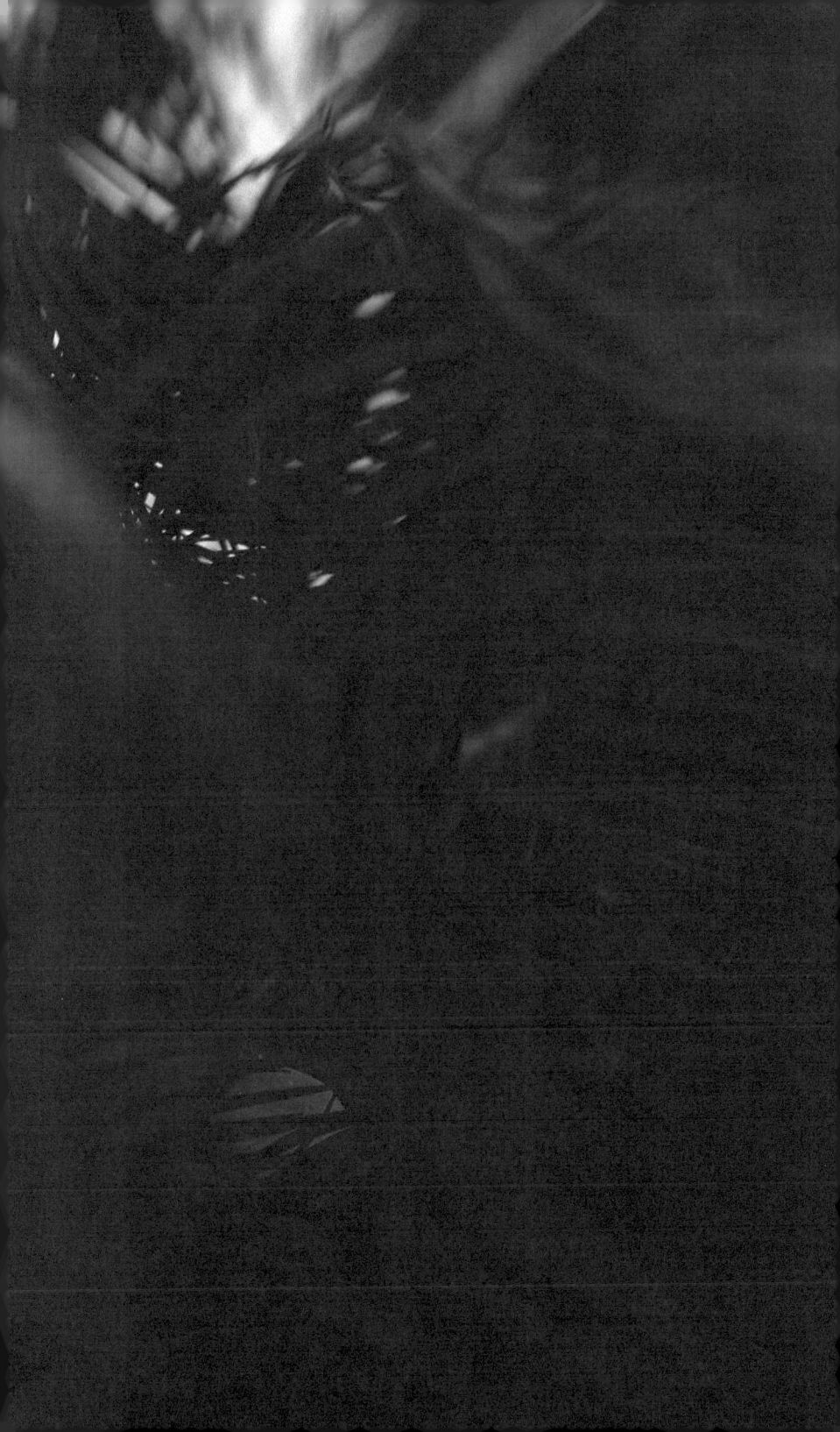

name: concrete[i]land

year: 2015

location: Makkasan, Bangkok, Thailand

pathology: narcissistic personality disorder

prop: 600 ceramic components
\ robotic RSI-perturbation extrusion
\ site-extracted mud
\ steel & concrete structure \\ permanent

duration: 12:00

pitch: | bonfire spot | lost-memory alchemy
operative mode of sub-sub-culture echoes

/// mud-dirt-turd / human matters in a loop / substances
in their states of chemical transformation and uses /
from the fruit of the earth to their rejection / faeces
/   celebrate   waste   garbage
excrements / all      around perspiring
and taking shape   /   extracted-
pumped-remixed-   extruded / from
the   digestive   belly village /
open sky sewage   under pilotis /
now piling up   on the visible
level /// within   g e n e t i c a l l y -
diseased autarky   /   island   of
degeneration / they said // social contract / an
unstable oral work in progress /// vs the idiocratic
upper regime where language has been reduced to a daily
life commerce / routine of merchandising / in self-
congratulation for words' disappearance //// deep back
inside // books are exchanged through their ashes /
take a shot / sniff condensed particles / in suspense
/// a kind of cultural methadone / easily-accessible
stirring stifling barely-bearable immersive-emotional
self-suggested ///

*Around 33% of the urban population in the developing world in
2012, or about 863 million people, lived in slums. New York
City is believed to have created the world's first slum, named
Five Points in 1825. Those territories could be described
as zones of non-droit, informal economy, criminal seeds and
organisation, or on the other hand as a bottom-up economy and
politics, through local neighbourhood negotiations and the re-
questionning of power delegation, depending on which side you
find yourself to be.*

27

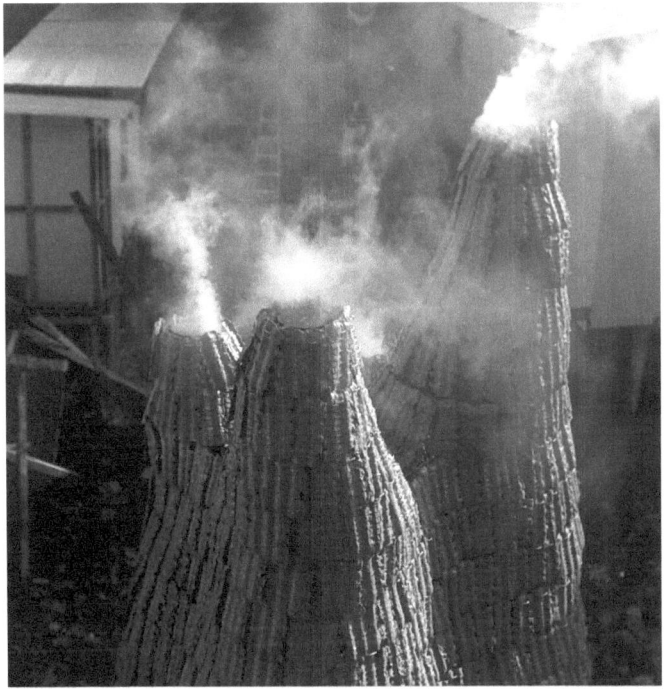

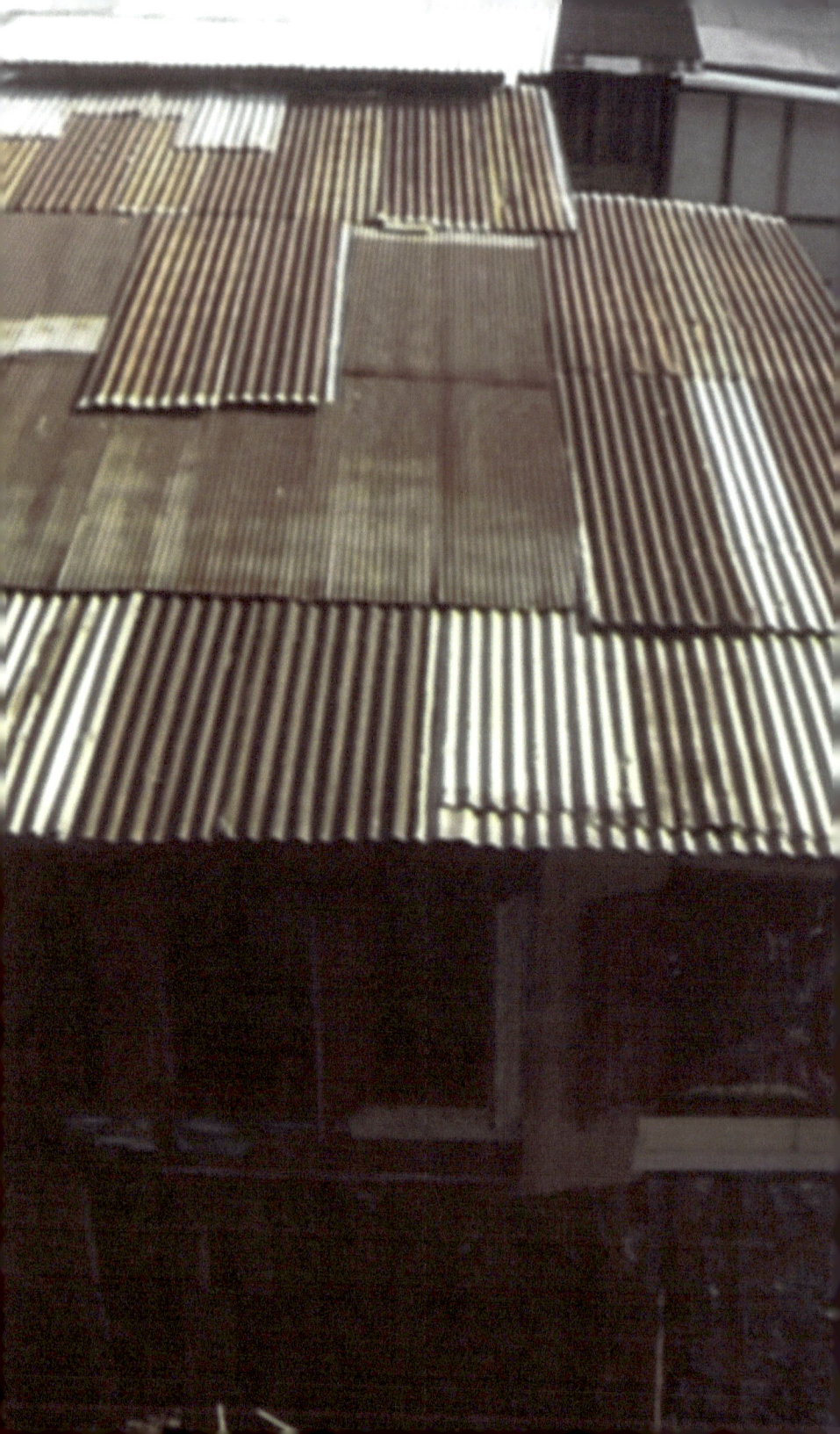

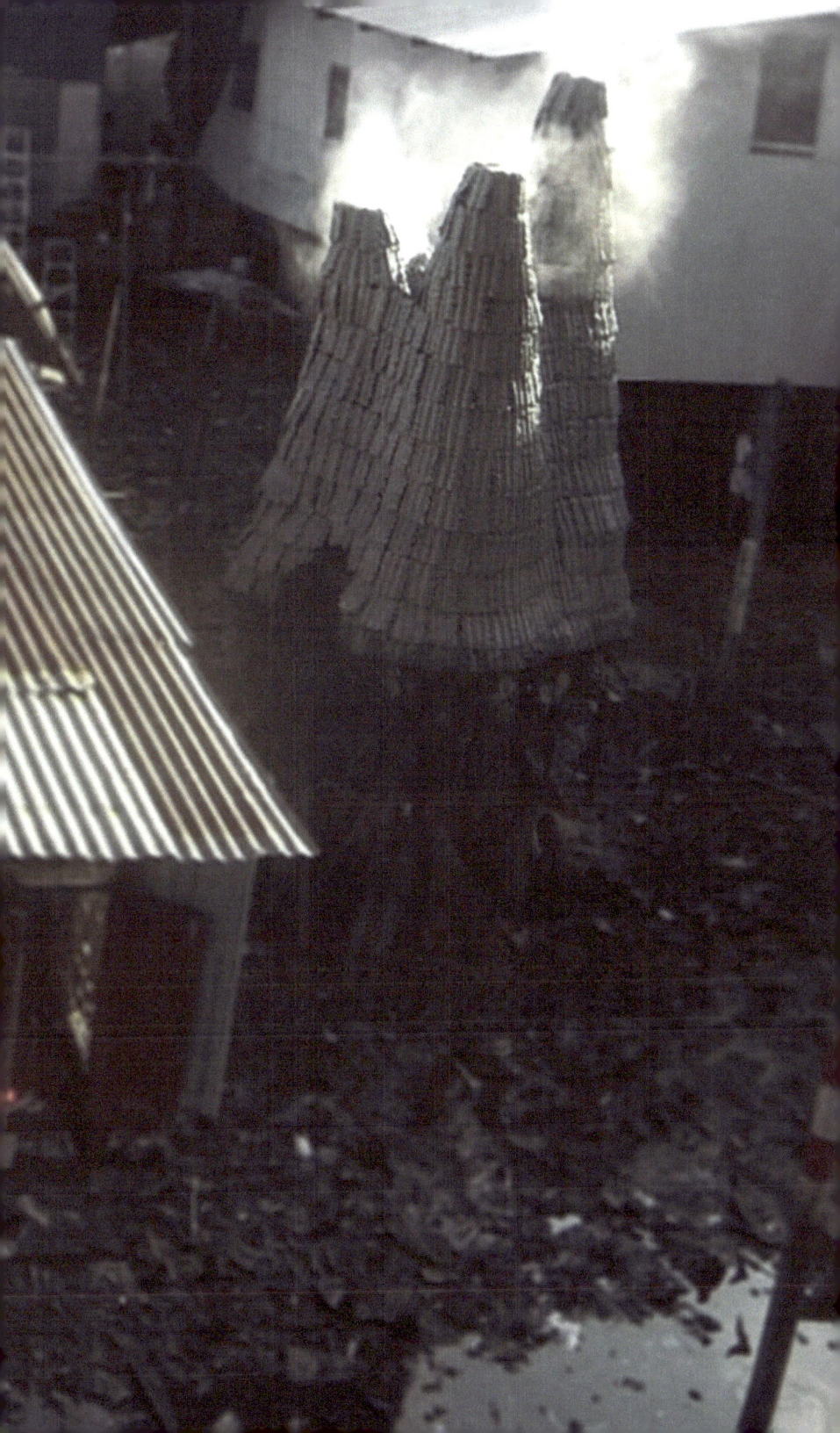

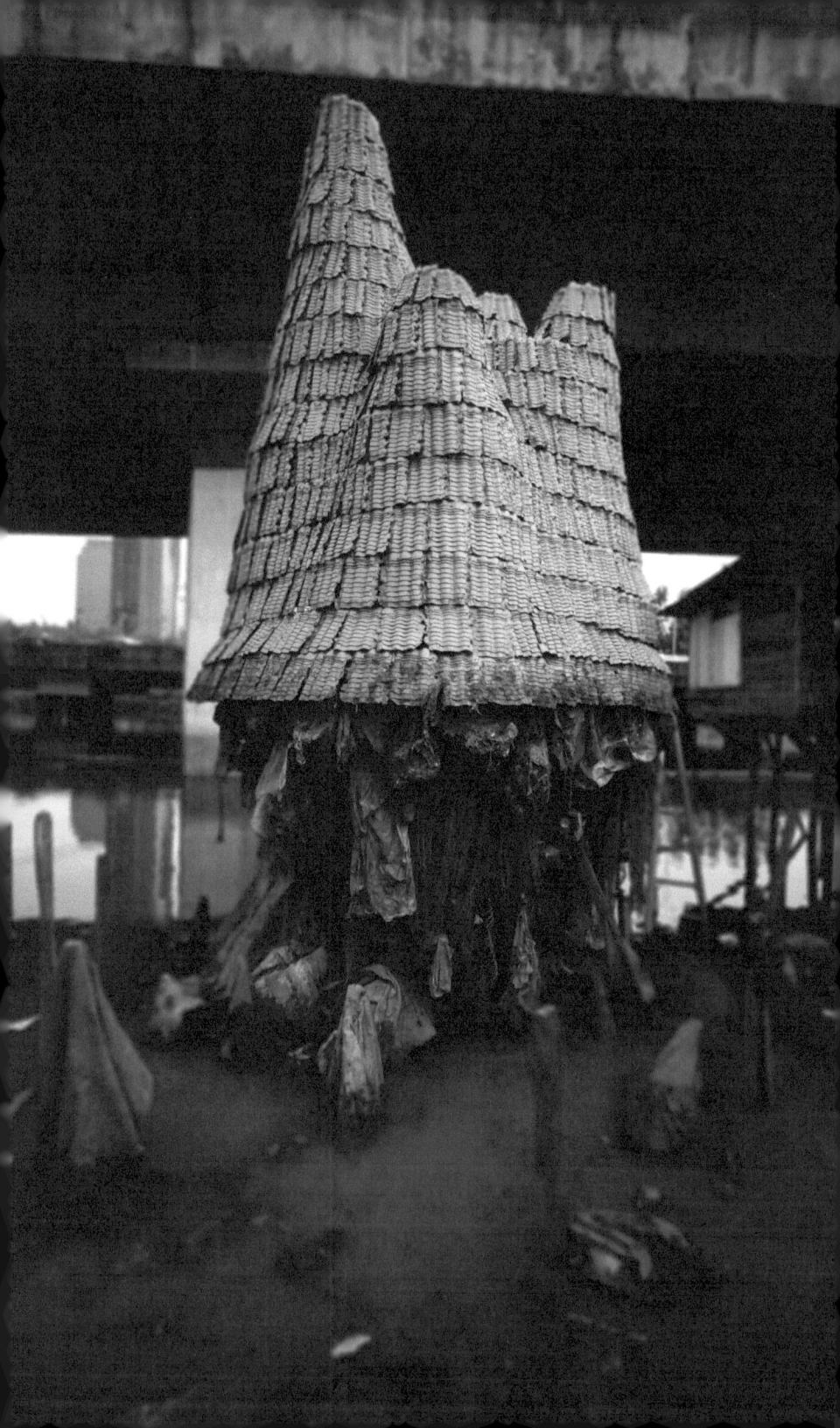

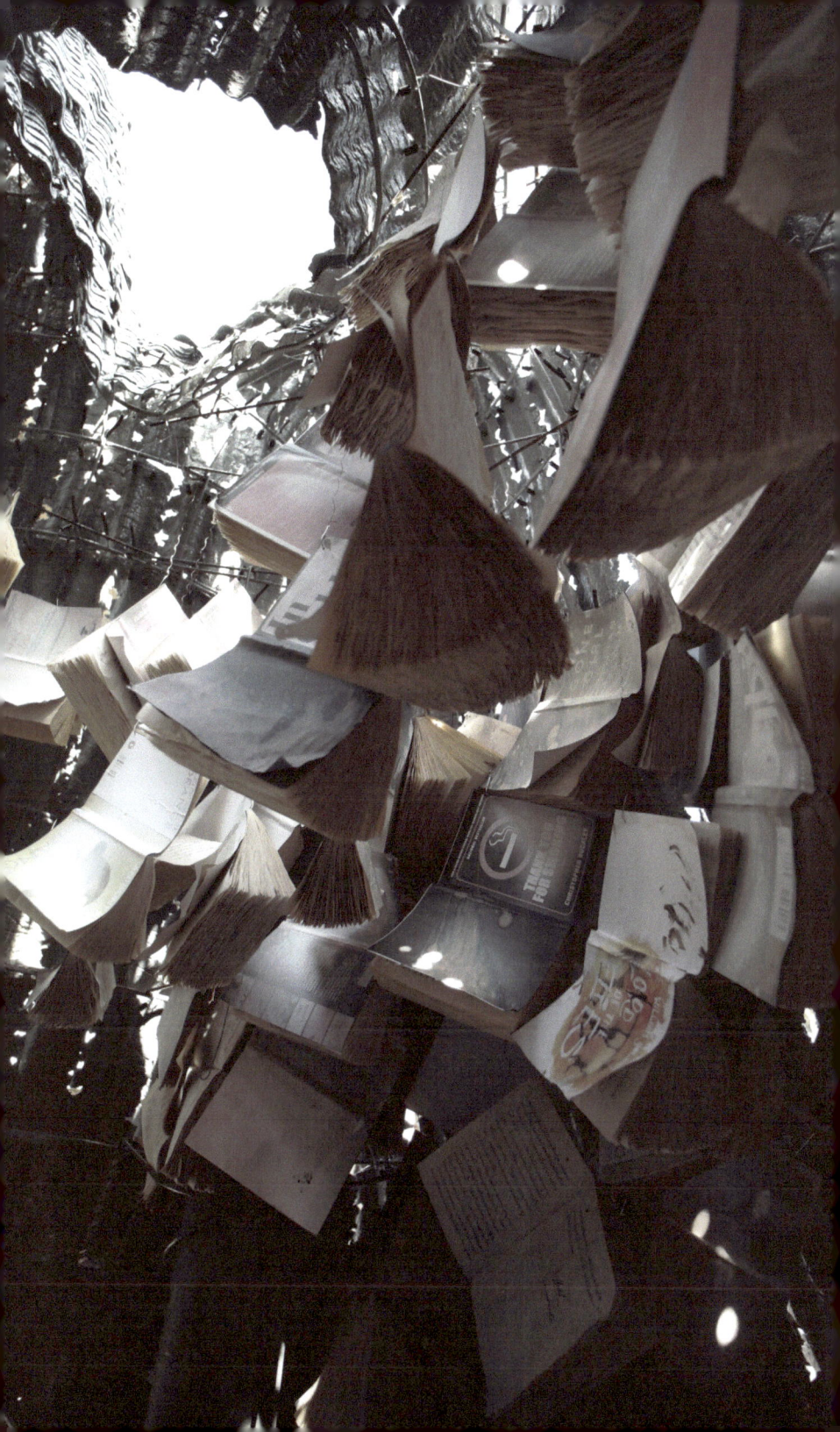

name: ... Would Have Been My Last Complaint

year: 2012

location: Gokarna, India

pathology: paraphrenia

prop: 250 site-extracted crafted laterite stones
\ 250 blown-glass components
\ verrucaria nigrescens \\ permanent

duration: 11:44

pitch: a self-indulgent exhibitionist
| embassy |

/ it would have been the last / leaving my condition
unresolved / i would have felt ///// showing myself
powerless / despite my
knowledge // or  because of it
//// now waiting for the believers
// to validate my tears and
my weakness / testimony of my
self-complaisant- trap // the last
complaint / to renegotiate
common sense / the 'sufficient
reason' / the hypothesis of
living together /// they are late ///

This antagonism between believers and philosophers is
instrumentalized, according to some, as a civilization war
alibi. BUT. Remember the debate during the Enlightenment
between Diderot and Kant, between the construction of knowledge
from the sciences to the notion of the sublime ... from the
Encyclopaedia to the Black Forest, from the philosopher Sri
Ganapati Vedeshwar, living in Gokarna, to the Community of
Hindu Believers. A true story.

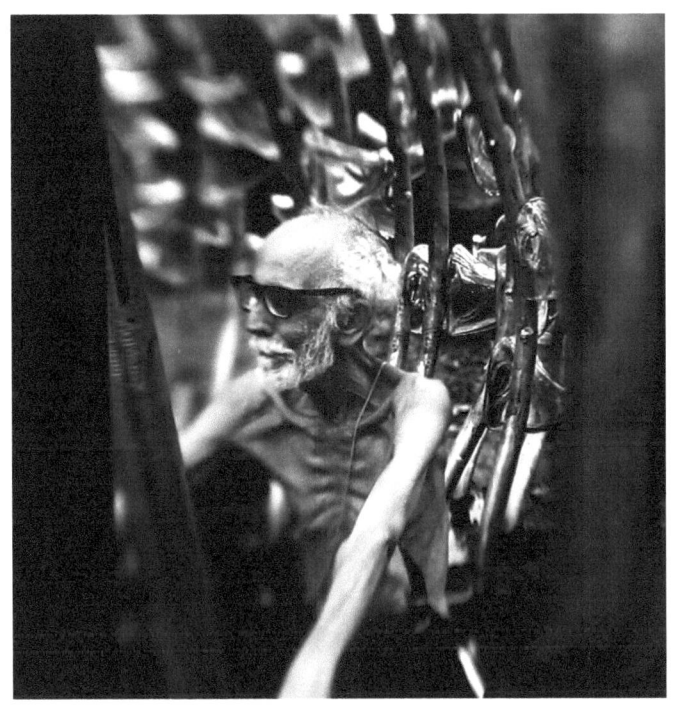

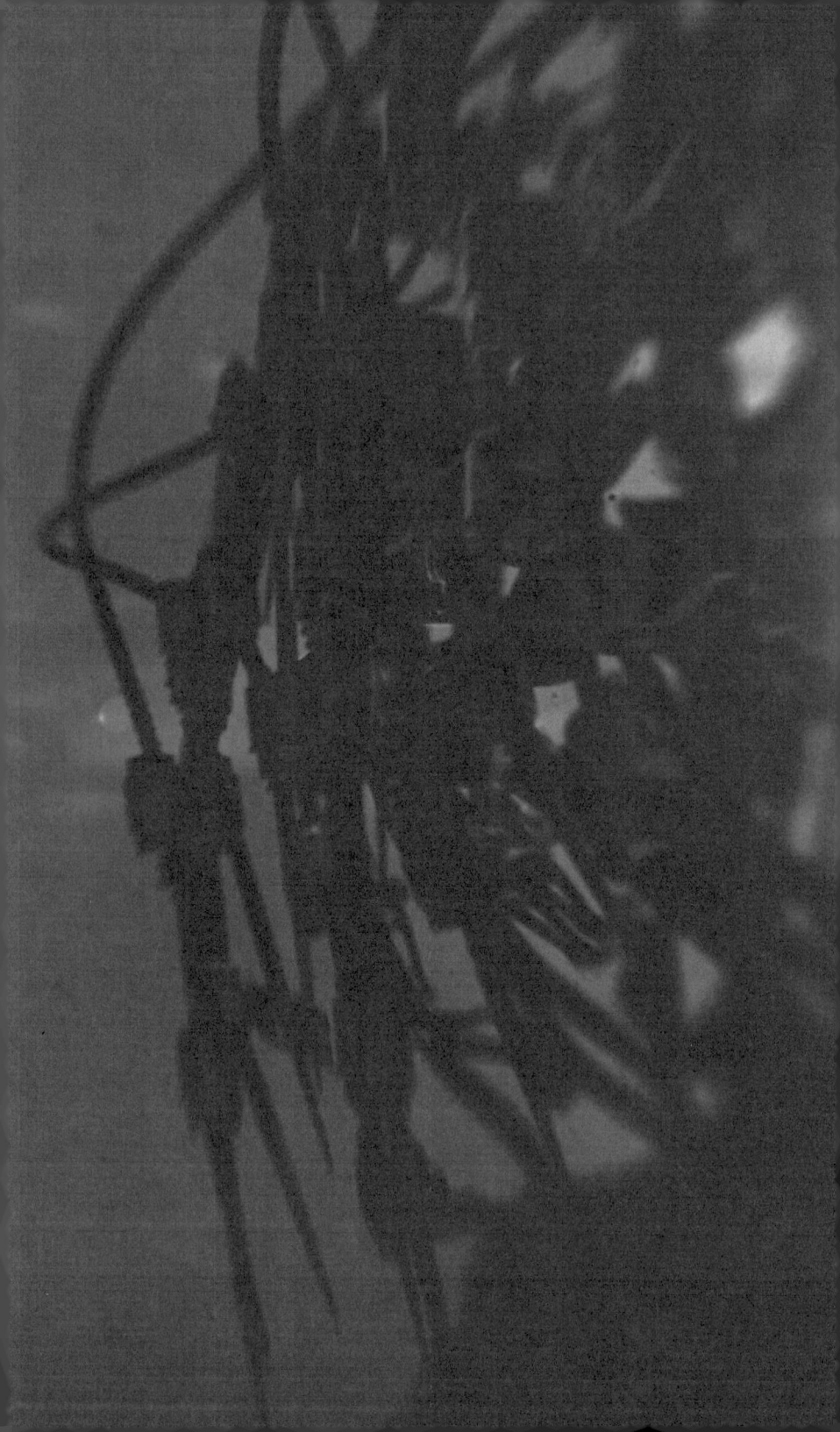

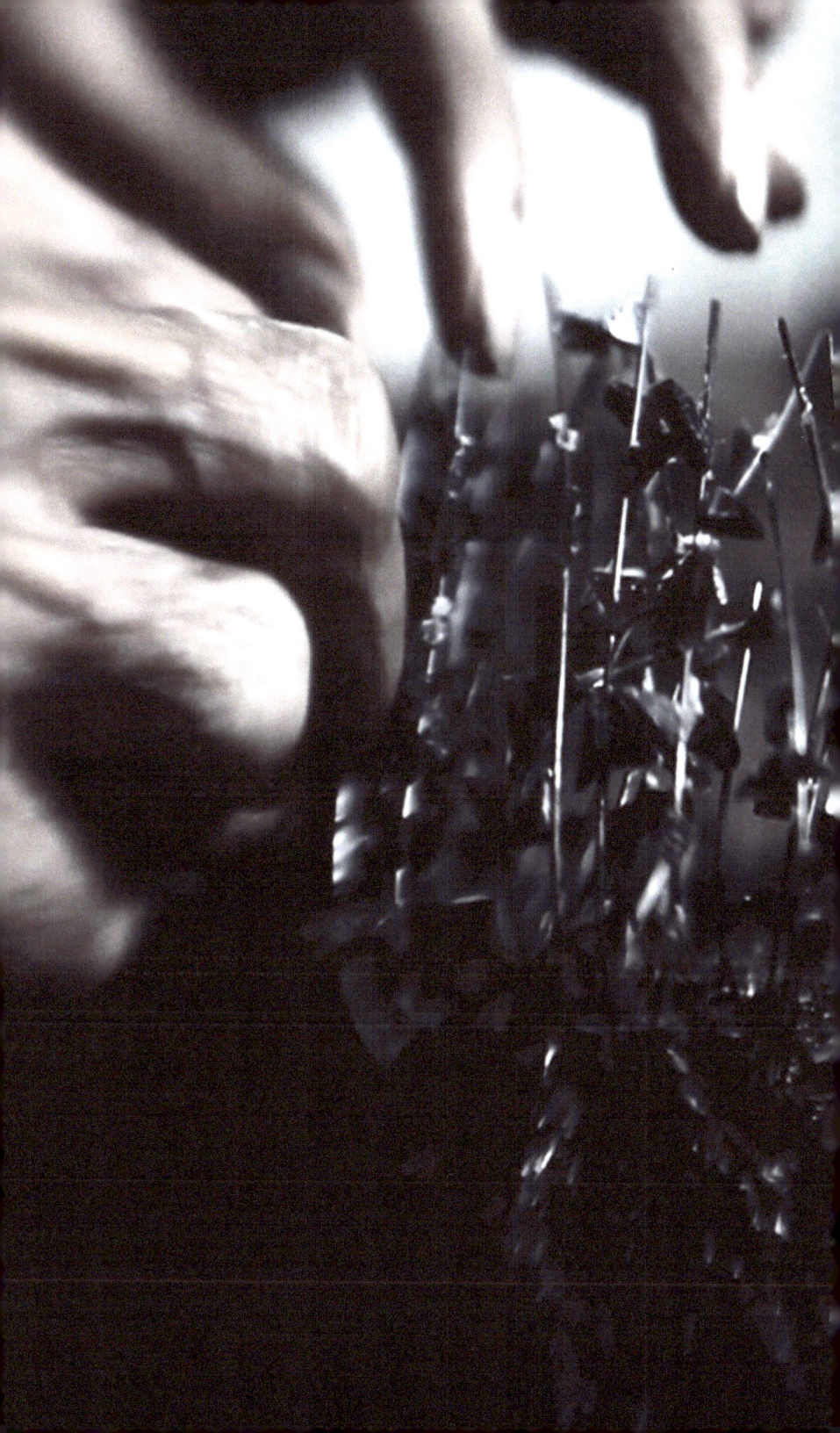

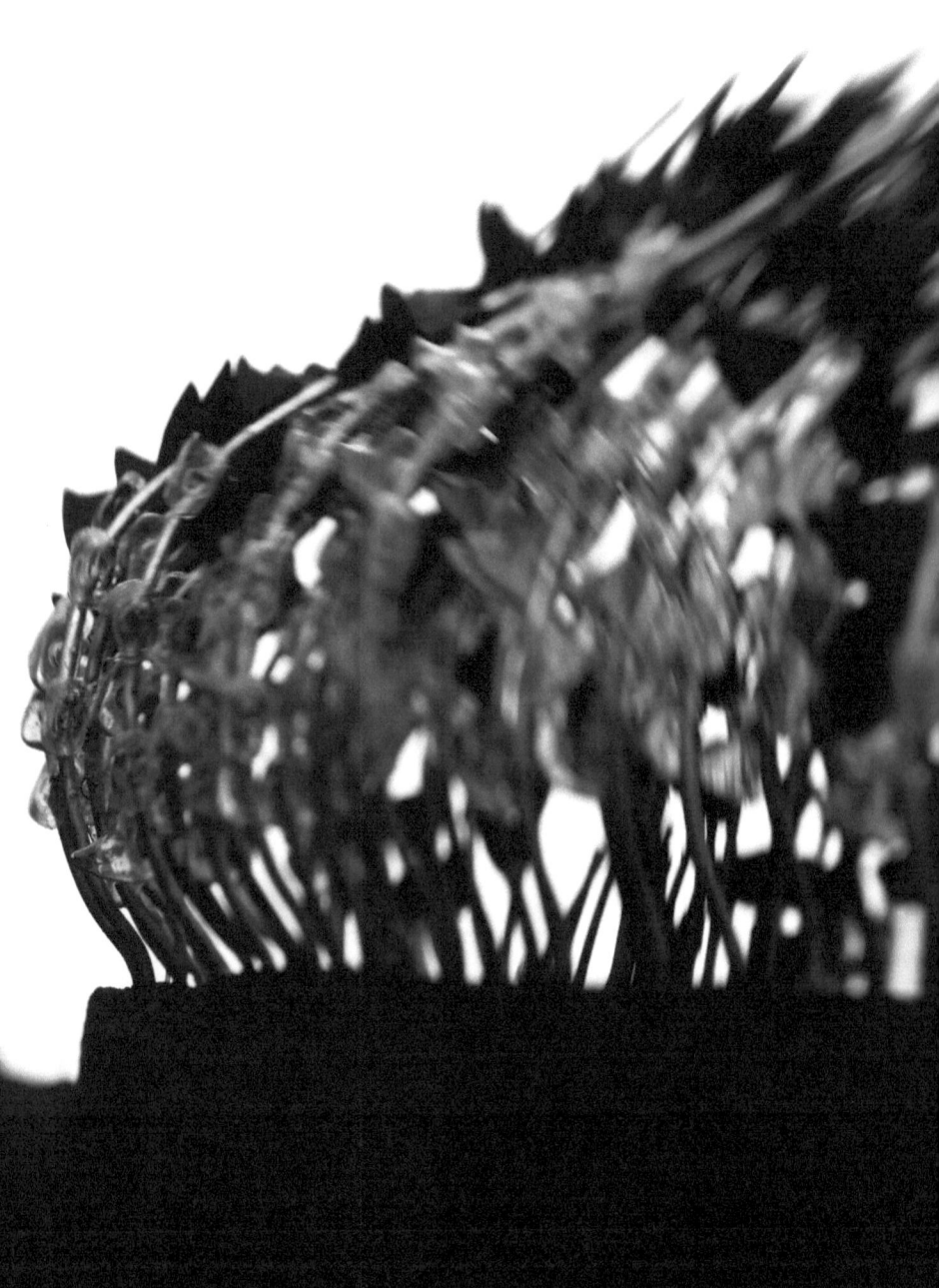

name: La Passe

year: 2013

location: Boutox, France

pathology: repression

prop: 800 linear meter site-extracted pine timber \ copper-silver ionized water \ geotextile \\ permanent

duration: 01:00

pitch: penitence | tub | for a psychoanalyst

/ psycho zones / me-masochist / pleonasm / professional discharge / no-more / occupational disease / eros and thanatos drives / a constant (mis)thrust / defiance of the wild / repressed desires of the man in the  tree / waiting for me / triggering my own frustration / so long … / a life of voluntary ignorance / it's time now / retroactive self-punishment / from coitus interruptus / guilty / i'm guilty to drown / in the wood / tub / from my own forest / property / swallowing the chalice at each breaststroke / 'all in you is dried up' /

In the 1960s, Lacan was increasingly occupied with two intersecting themes: the issue of how to define and assess the end of a psychoanalysis, and the question of the relationship between psychoanalysis and science. The Pass (La Passe) is a procedure he introduced in 1967 as a means of gathering data on a psychoanalysis and investigating its results.

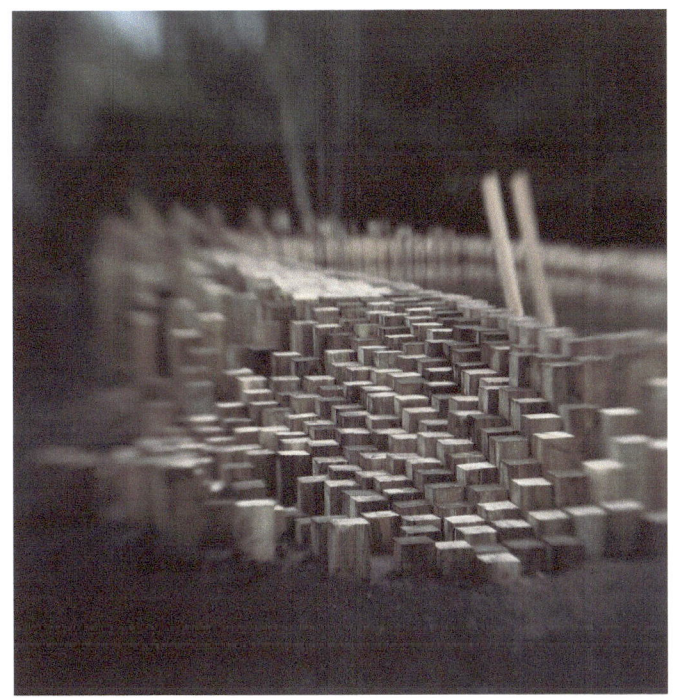

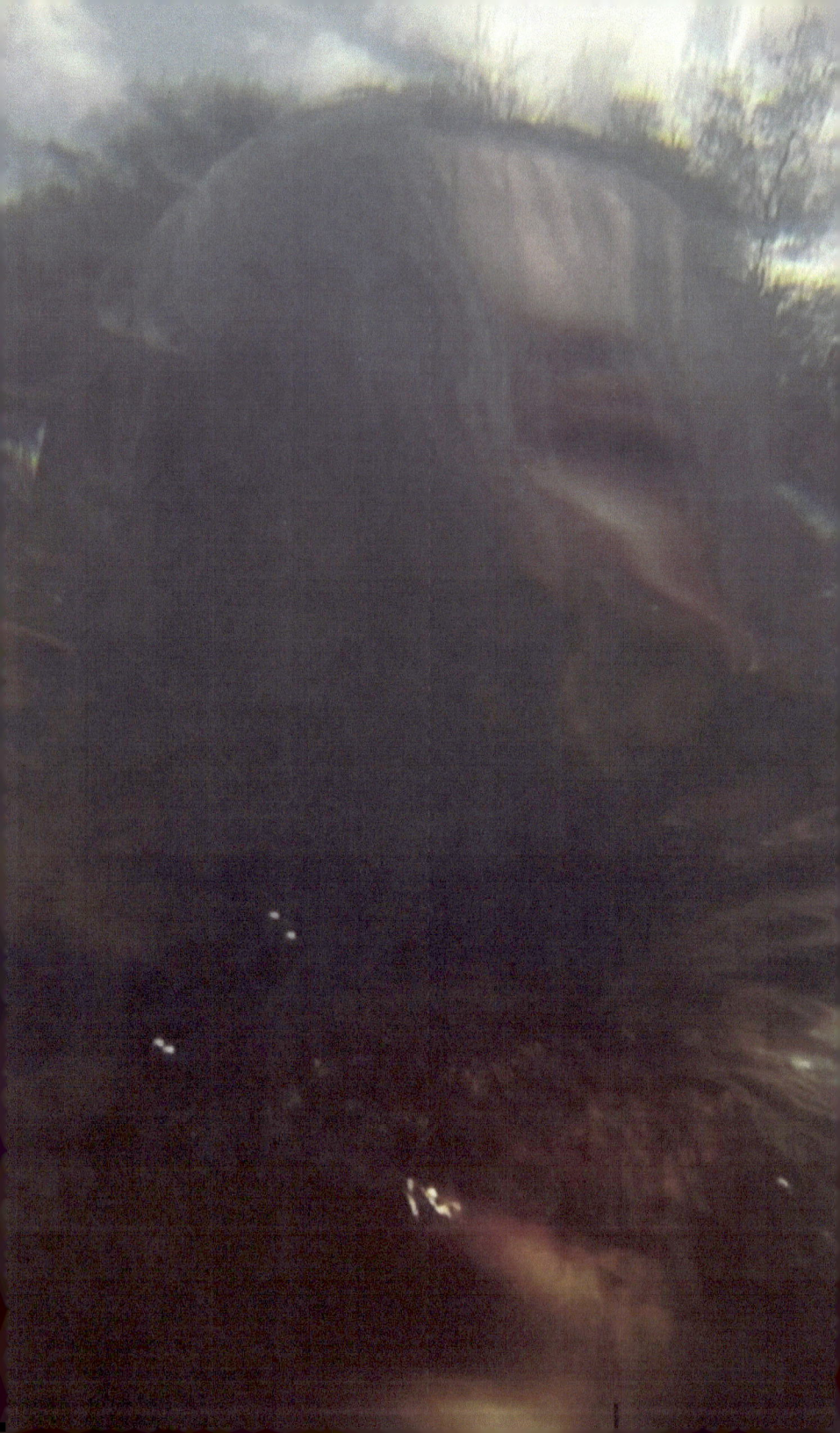

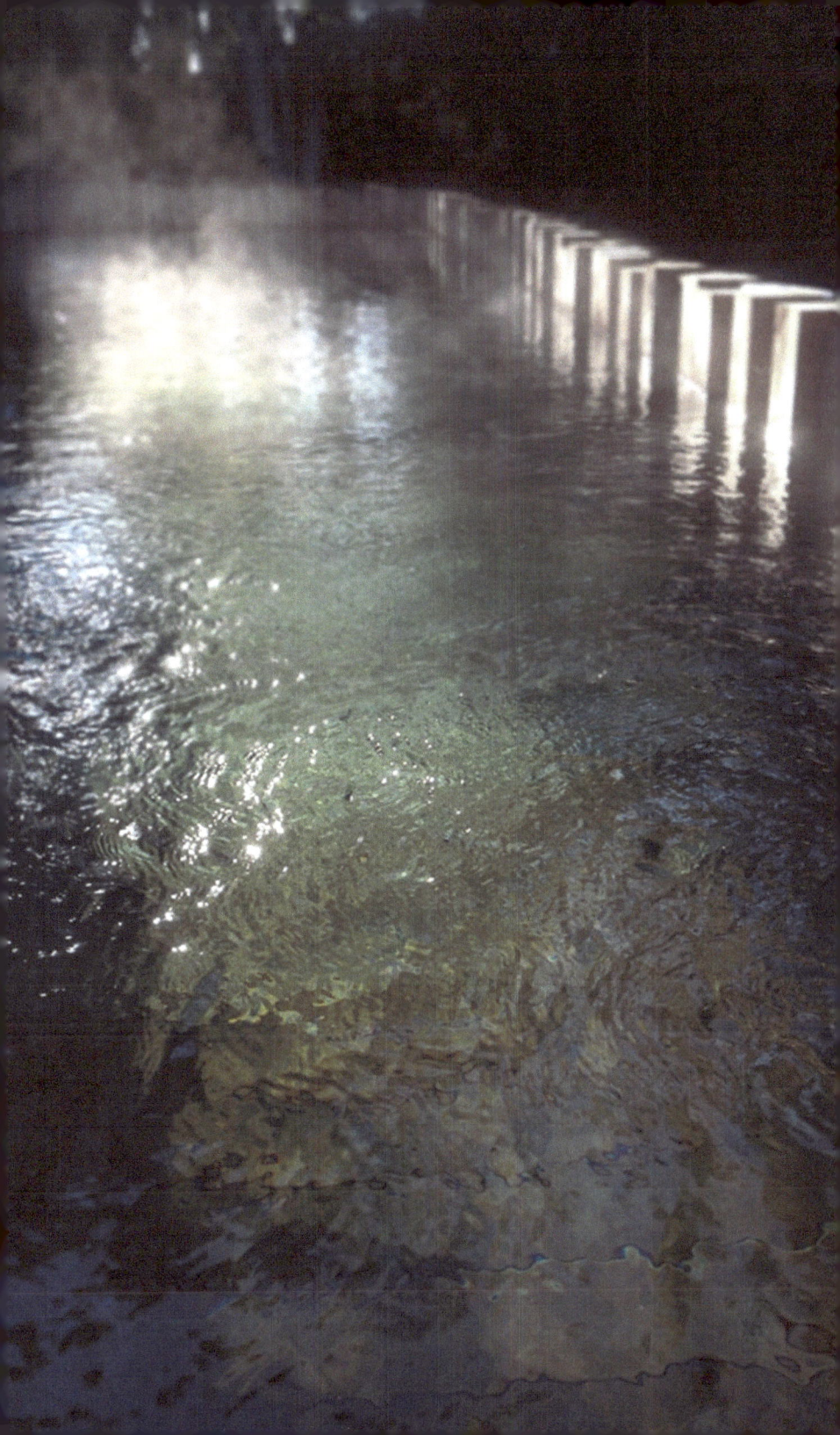

name: the Offspring

year: 2014

location: Kwai River, Kachanaburi, Thailand

pathology: instinctual incest

prop: 6 woven living bamboo clusters
\ 300 bio-plastic leaves \\ until decay

duration: 10:00

pitch: forbidden experiment | lab |

/ i a female / i the subject of your studies / i a
feral child / i civilization's nightmarish phantasm /
i a construct / an anti-dote / the haunted reject / i
have nothing to do with nature // i always mediated /
under scrutiny / i living proof of non-objectivity / of
the experiment's  observer affect-
effects / i your tacit desires
/ i your errant consciousness /
i the reasons you invented to avoid
feeling it /// i the offspring of
so-called science neutrality /
i no milgram guinea pig / i
civilization's d i s c o n t e n t s
//////// i h y s t e r i a
possession trouble / i no voice but a scream / no word
but a whisper / i naïve and obscene / i possessed and
in trance // i deal in charms spells and instincts ////
and i will not mimic your supremacist manners / i the
disorder to come / animist / floating with the spirits
/ the devil inside / its power arouses / and what you
called incest will grow /

*A language deprivation experiment, also called "The Forbidden
Experiment", consists in isolating infants from ordinary human
contact and especially from the normal use of spoken or signed
language in the hope of discovering the fundamental character
of human nature or the origin of language. Although not
designed to study language, similar experiments on non-human
primates (the "Pit of Despair") utilising complete social
deprivation resulted in psychosis.*

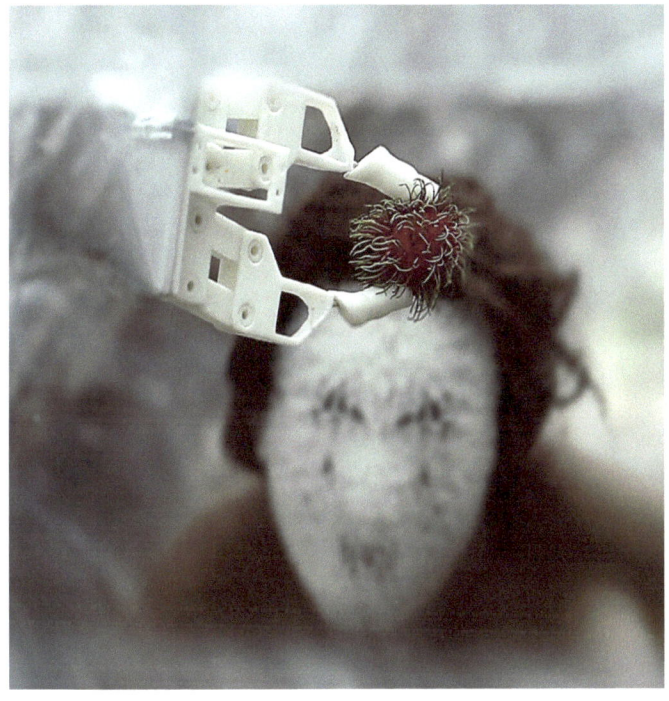

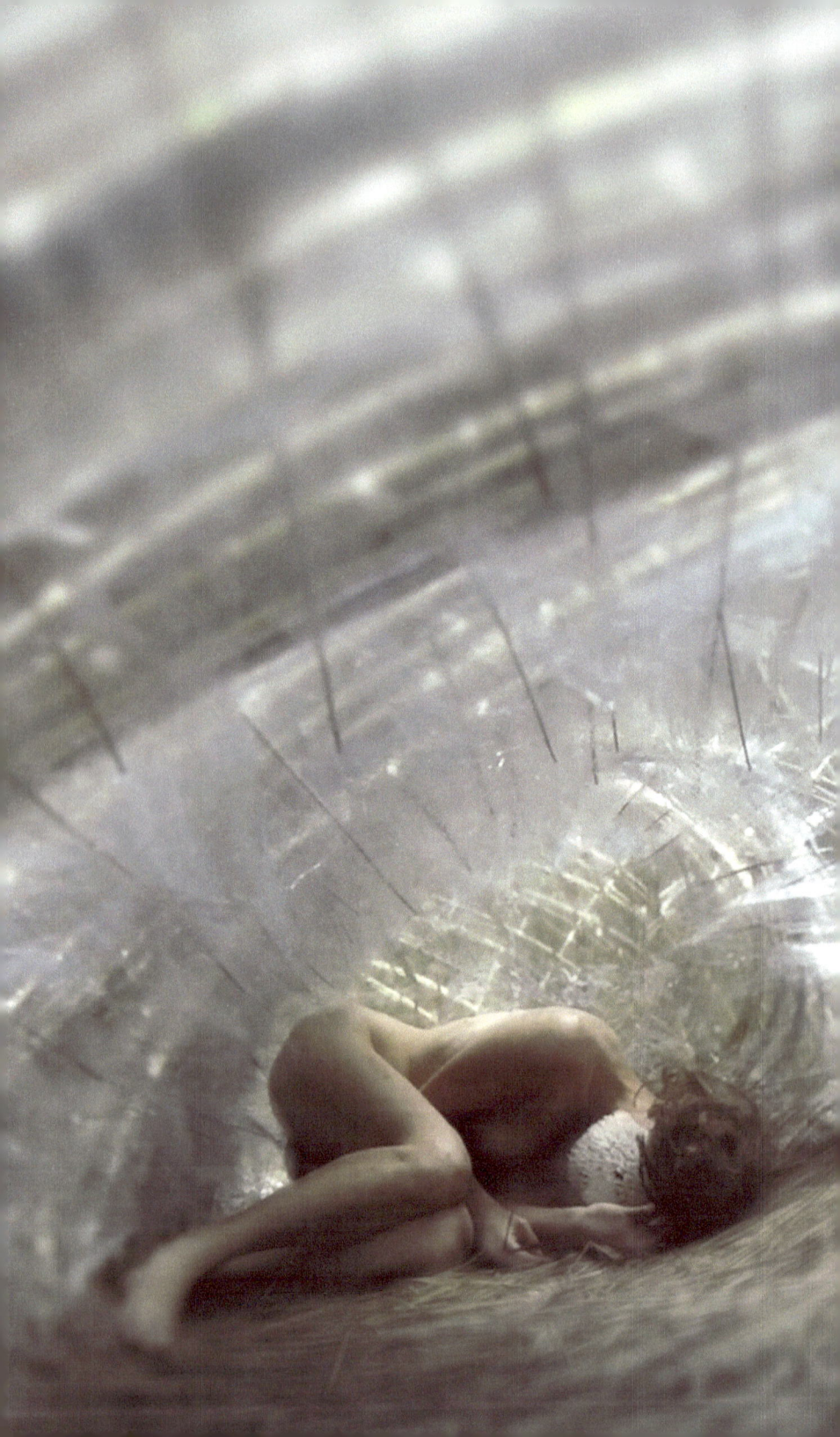

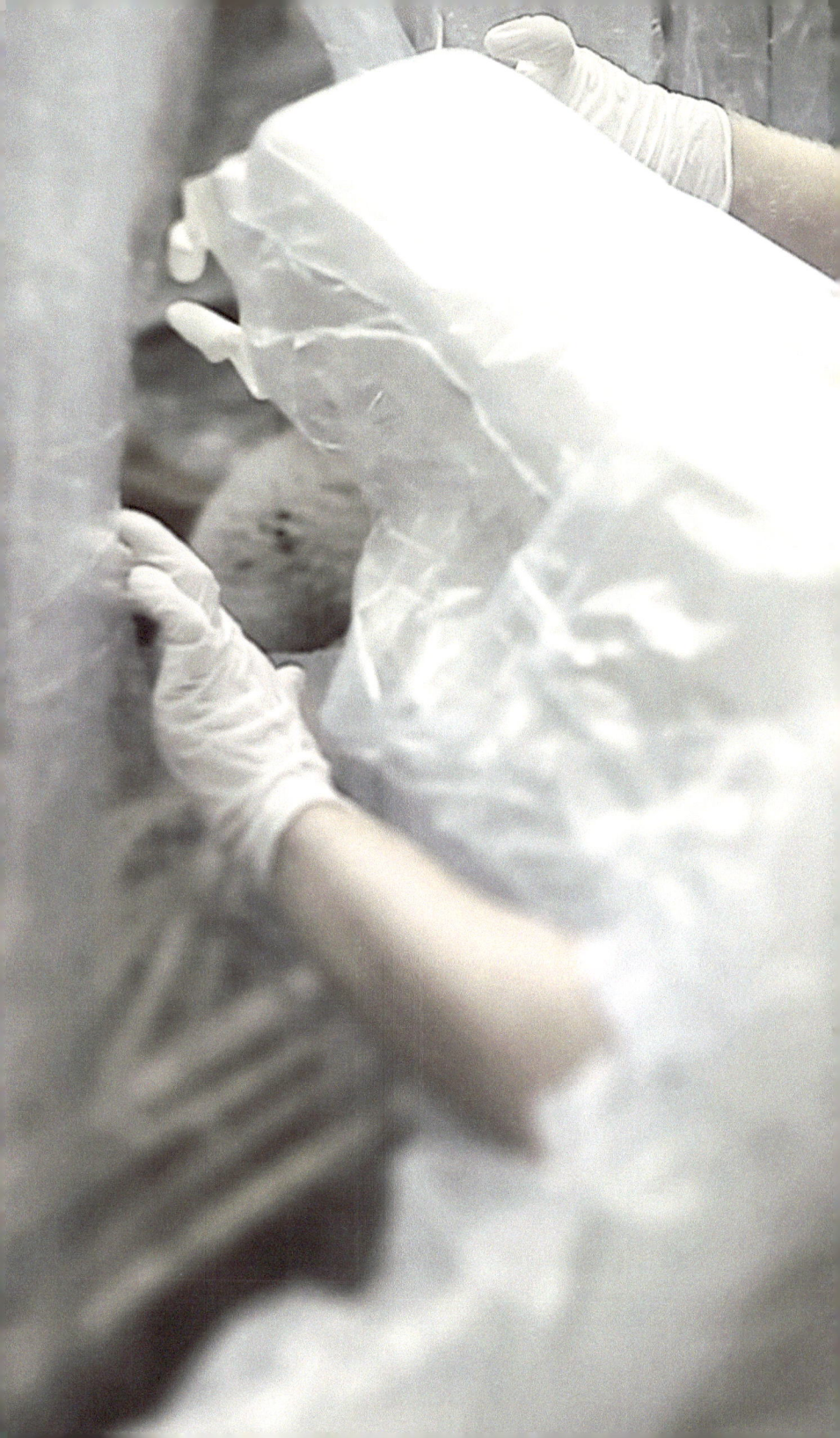

name: altered state

year: 2012

location: Krems an der Donau, Austria

pathology: pavlovian pheromonal trouble

prop: hot-wire-cut polystyrene foam
                           \ diffusion pump \ chemical blowers
                     \ androstanol & estratetraenol pheromones
                                \\ itinerant exhibition piece

duration: 01:00

pitch: limitless chemical | trap |
                     of 'air loom' daughters under influence

/ between us and the world / emotional delivery /
synthesis of a pregnant woman's pee / what makes
addiction / smelling mesmerism /// the line of physio-
s u b j e c t i v i t y   /   reptilian
brain escapes /   crossing   real-
unreal   boundary      and   atavism   /
logic and illogic   // it knows the
viscera   the   arterials   and
the   headless   desirable machine
or   human   body   ////// it plays
the   puppet's   free will / the
impetus // weaves   airs into a warp
of magnetic fluid / pneumatic chemistry crossbred with
animal magnetism / fuelled by a combination of fetid
effluvia / spermatic-anima-seminal rays / putrid human
breath / horse's anus' gas / brain-saying and dream-
working // stinks up the de-darwinist room /

*The Air Loom (1810) was a mind control device capable of
remotely manipulating the thoughts of its victims. James
Tilly Matthews, a Bedlam inmate, believed that a gang of
criminals and spies skilled in pneumatic chemistry had taken
up residence at London Wall and were tormenting him by means of
rays emitted by a machine, via "Lobster-cracking", preventing
the circulation of the blood by a magnetic field, "Stomach-
skinning", and "Apoplexy-working with the nutmeg grater",
involving the introduction of fluids into the skull. Matthews'
delusions had a definite political slant: this gang's chief
targets were leading government figures... by means of their rays
they could influence ministers' thoughts and read their minds.*

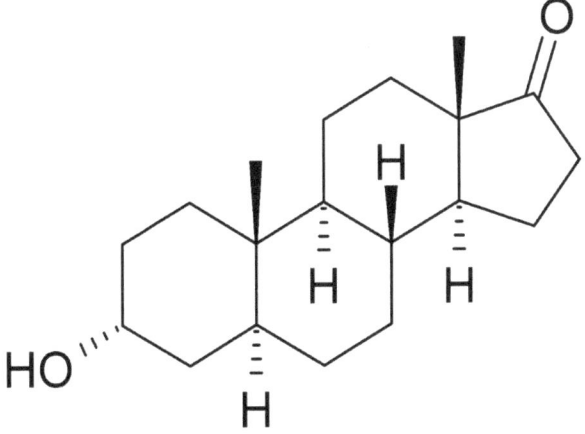

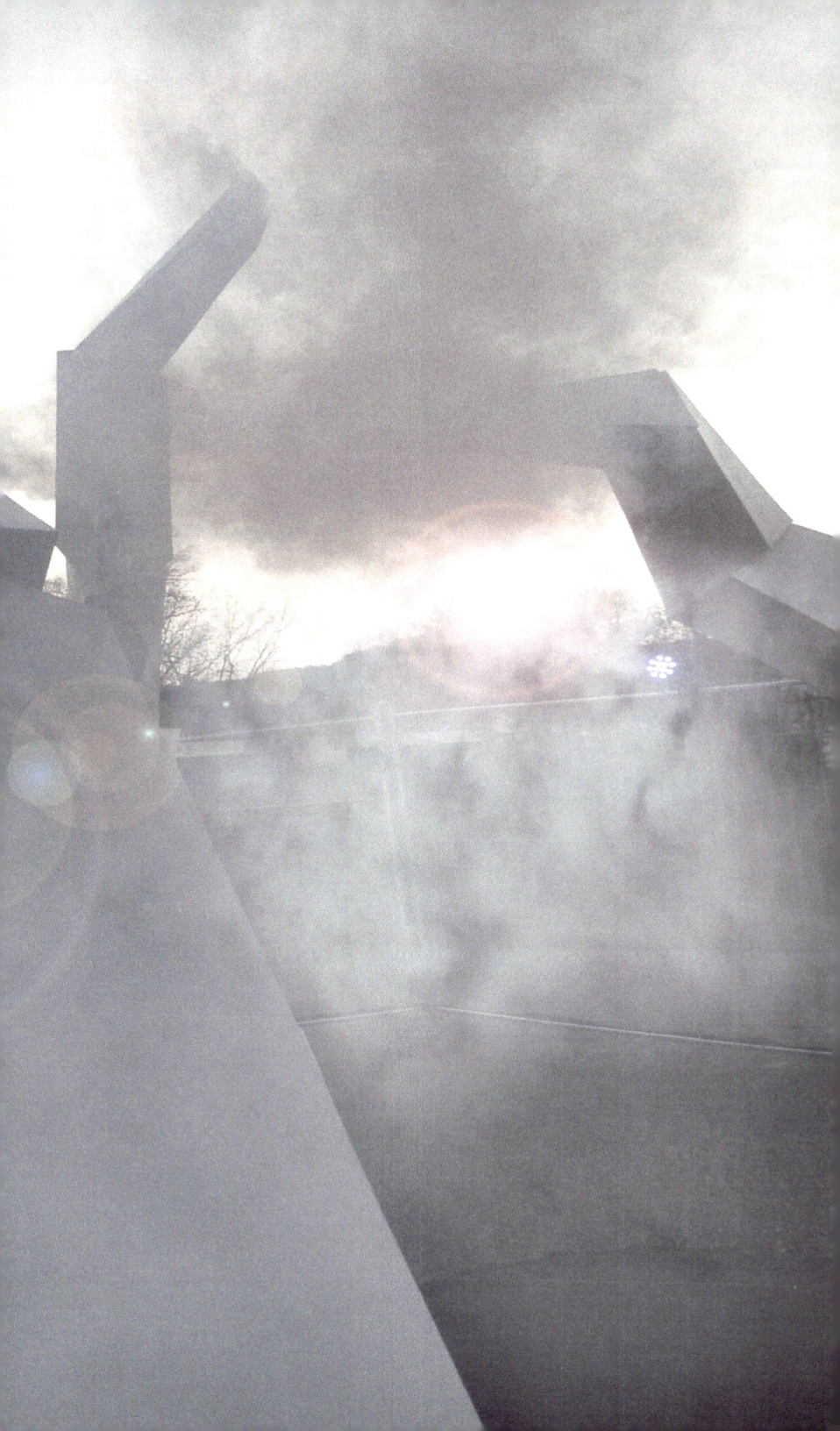

name: Feral Child (prelude)

year: 2013

location: Singapore

pathology: animist resistance

prop: bent dead black bamboo \ mud
                              \\ 1-week butoh performance set

duration: 03:59

pitch: | self-protection biotopes |

// regression to wilderness as a self-decameron / a solitude gate for the 'last human' in singapore // rejection of hygienic proto-fascist urbanism // mowgli syndrome /// displays a reasonable lack  of interest in the human activity around / seems mentally affected // high degree of acculturation / to survive in hostile situations /// bunker- department- stored city // plaintive fearful behaviour / whispering sounds reminiscent of jungle animal groans /// please do not disturb and do not feed her / we are not quite yet in a zoo //

Butoh, which can be executed with or without an audience, originating from the early movement of ankoku butō ("dance of darkness"), arose within Japanese society after WWII, following a mixture of confusion, caused by the industrialization process of their millenary traditional culture, and horror, caused by the bombs over Hiroshima and Nagasaki. The form was built on a vocabulary of crude physical gestures and uncouth habits… a direct assault on the refinement (miyabi) and understatement (shibui) so valued in Japanese aesthetics.

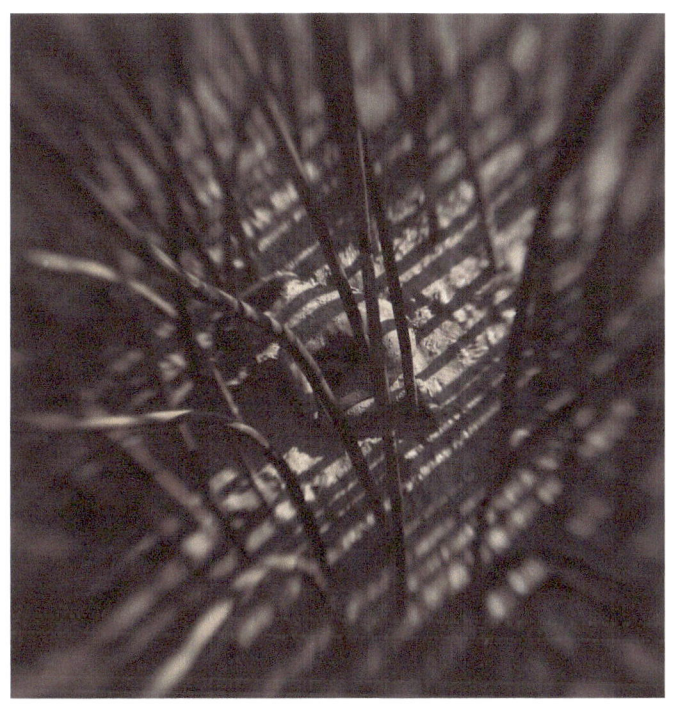

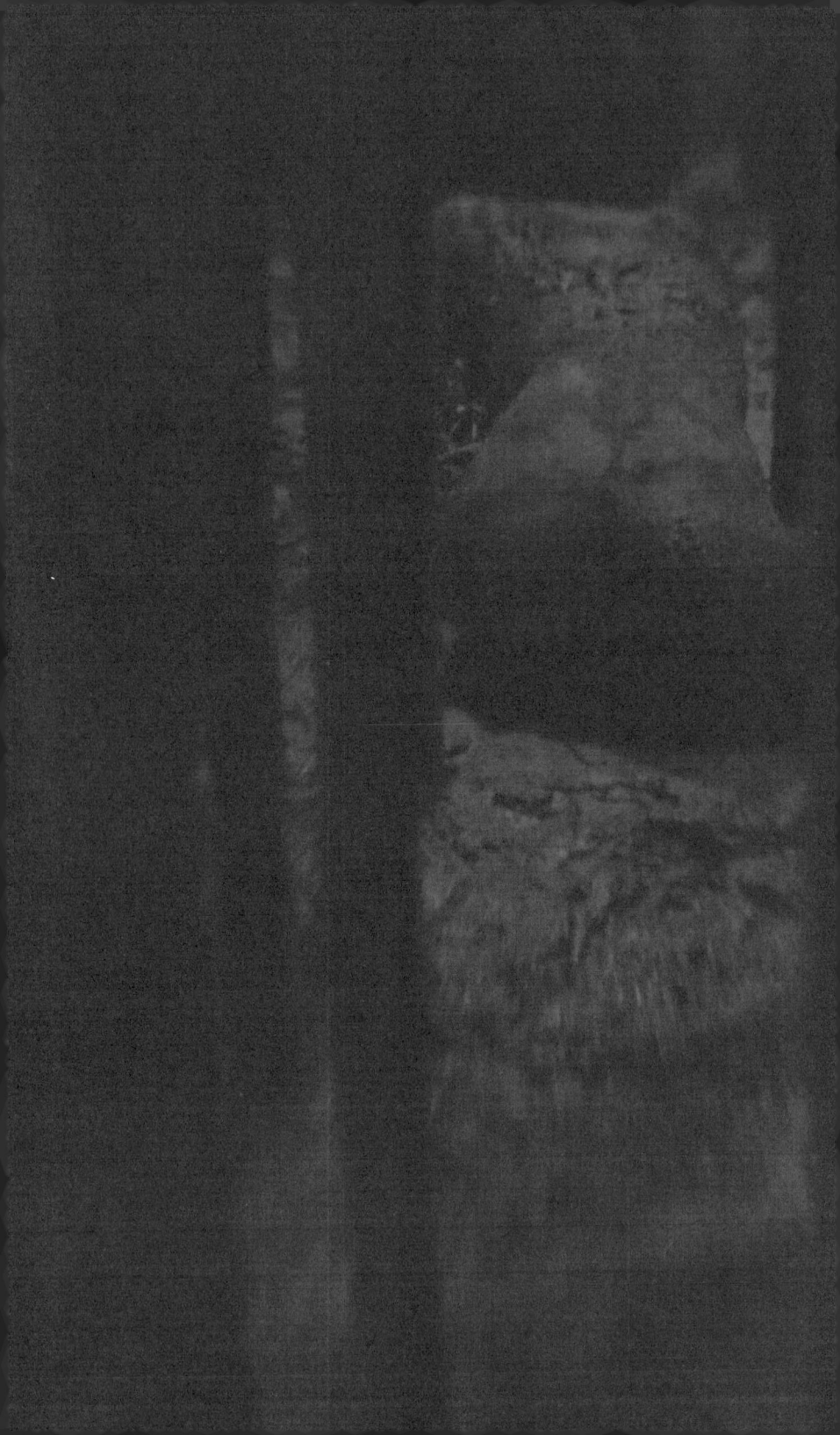

name: Σ d a y s

year: 2014

location: Bangkok, Thailand

pathology: paranoid identification

prop: 500 laser-cut aluminum sheet
components of 5 different sizes
\\ 3 weeks

duration: 04:52

pitch: slaughtering | house | love affair

/ street neighbourhood contract / mutual respect of
differences / wildness from urban wilderness / animalism
come home / through the orifice ///////////// / we
are rat-trapped together / in co-
servitude / you  are my friend /
my leisure / my speech-sparring-
partner / and my food // why did
you trust me / i am a swamp vamp
cramp / a cannibal / i swallow you
/ you are locked in my projection
/ no escape / it's over and
over again /// the wait for the
next to come / first days' excitement / the encounter
/ one-way gutter to the trap / regularly contracted
and expanded // i swallow you indefinitely // abuse-
amusement routine / hungering mutualism / aesthetical
ideological identification / and permanent barbarism /

*Mutualism is the way two organisms of different species exist
in a relationship in which each individual benefits from the
activity of the other. The relationship can be of the service-
resource or service-service type … making their possible
conflict a mutual suicide.*

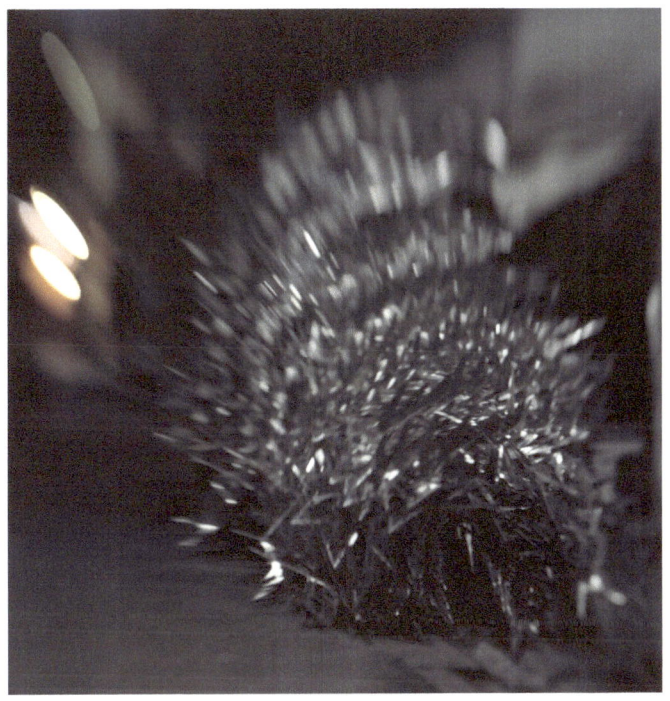

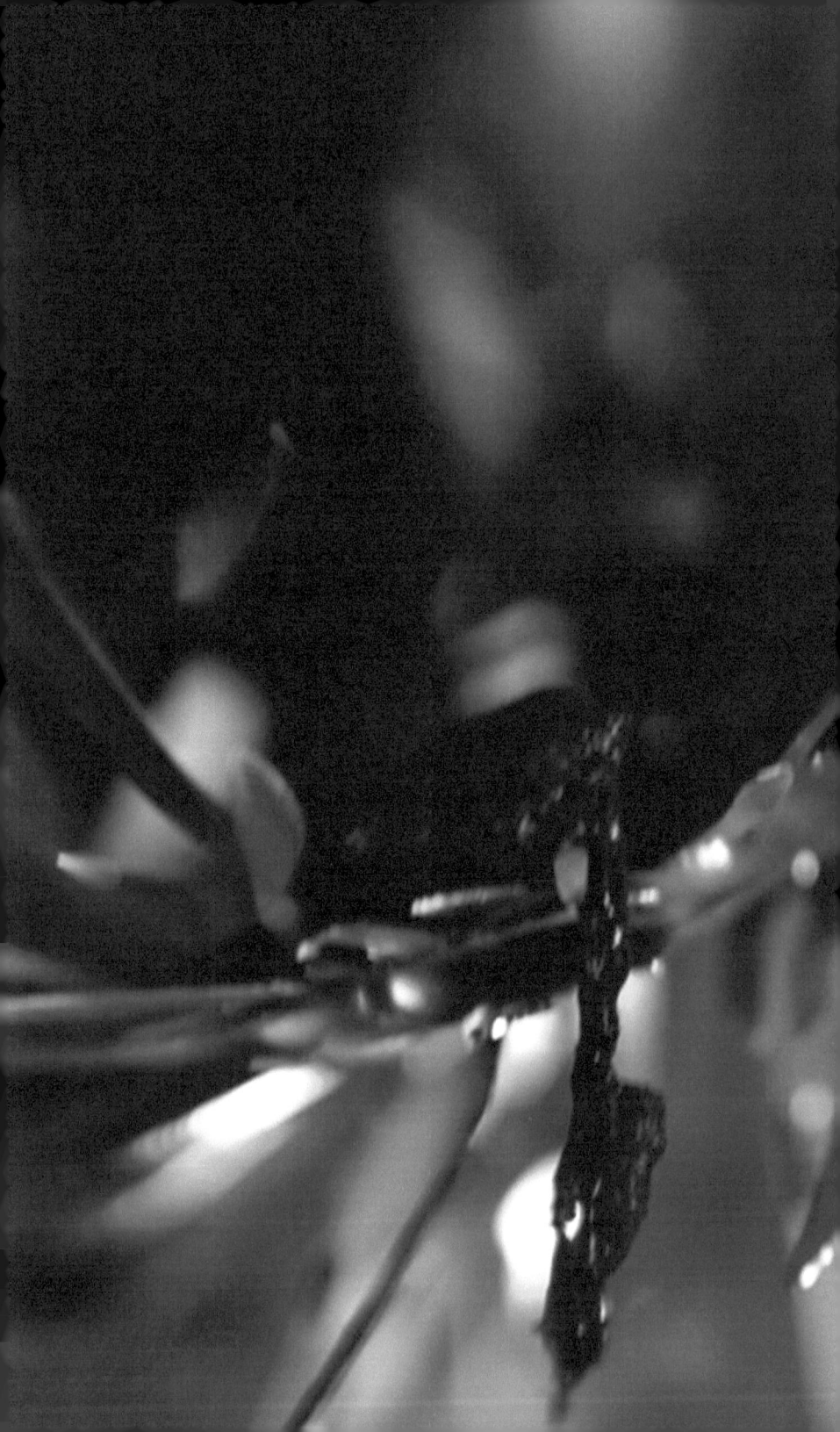

name: WHATEVS~4~EVS

year: 2014

location: Sathorn Unique, Bangkok, Thailand

pathology: grandiose delusions

prop: robotic-melted polystyrene foam
\ site-extracted dust \\ until decay

duration: 03:57

pitch: do not beam me up in a here&now
| concrete crack |

//// i am the fool // the banished king's jester
arbitrista midget // i am not a prophet and i am not
a merchant // i madly tell the truth and many other
jokes // main dwarf benefice ///// i want decay and your
love for decay // to see your grey insides / kiss your
fat and aborted  wrinkles // eat
your guilt and its permissions ////
i will lick your self-indulgence
and false moral contracts // and
i will penetrate the hole in your
head // the guts of your diseased
civilization // remain hidden in
there until the next decadence //
the next descent //// i am ready
now to become // decomposed matter // decayed skin //
eating the wall / the column // jailed and corroded
//// my king has left me again // in that ageless
structure / as your testimony // of such a sensible
era // living the money-moment / always subject to
change // stock-market-index-discourse //// the freak
show is perpetrated // yet where there once was joy //
now conformism // where there once was wit and burst
// now good intentions facebook friendships // my old
masters they knew how to puke defecate celebrate //
all were wrecked // master go jester remain //// no one
listening // of being / lost my reason ////

*The Jester Don Diego de Acedo is one of a series of portraits
by Diego Velázquez, transforming the tension and anxiety of the
Spanish court into a carnival freak show, a wounded, distorted,
and blemished representation of the human condition.*

*The Arbitristas were a group of reformers and writers in 17th-
century Spain, concerned about the decline of the economy.*

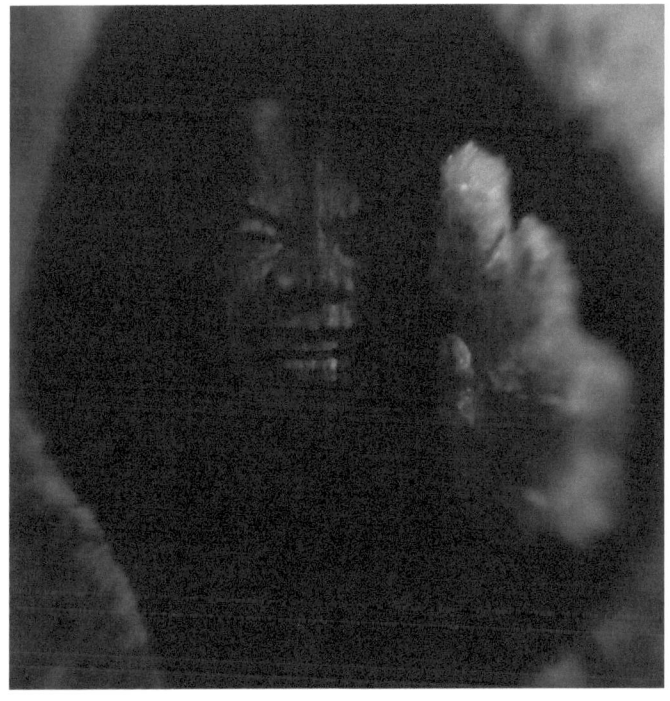

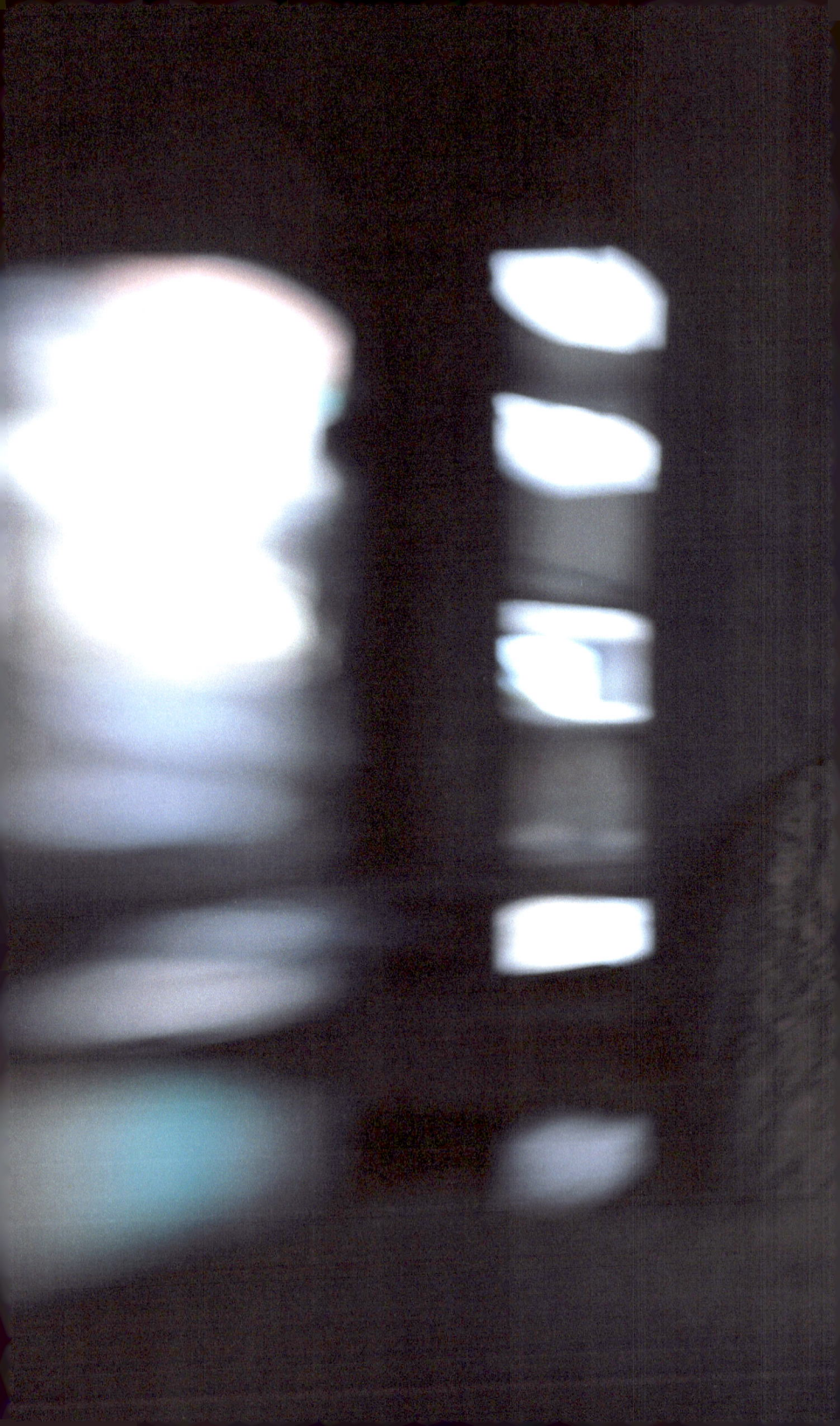

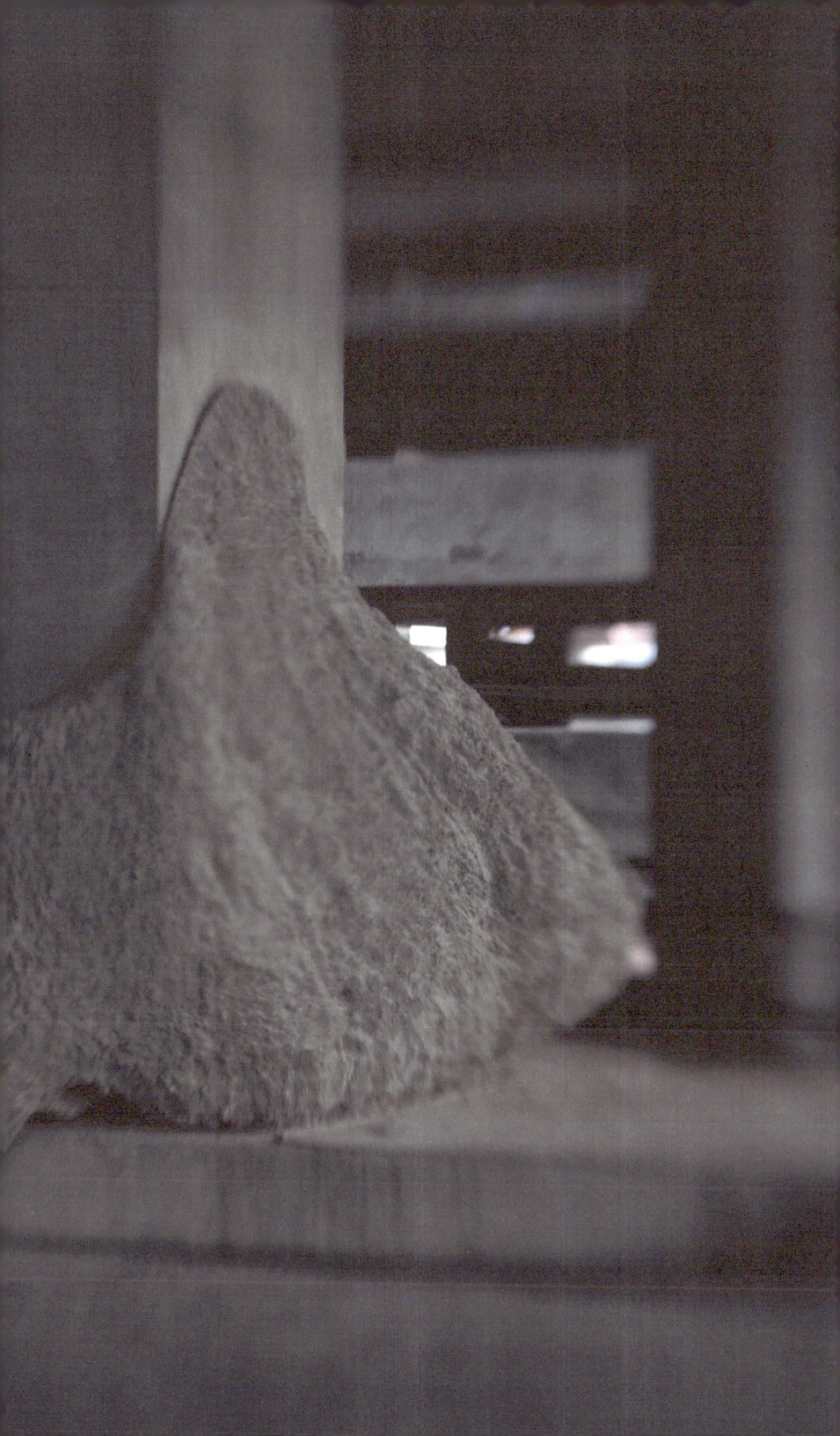

name: | what could happen |
Sanatorium's Last Call

year: 2015

location: Lej Nair, Switzerland

pathology: death drive

prop: 150 thermoformed bio-plastic components
\ site-extracted ice \\ until decay

duration: 12:04

pitch: safe self-sacrifice | landpark |

// a winter journey / every year / the train to the sanatorium // a ritual for the sane / the ones who have the right to die / old diseased sick deadening // for the young death is forbidden / not before we contribute // take the train every year / it sees us all age / decay / become grey // zombies on their last ride / always the last ride / and as they stuff themselves up / pretend to be the idiot / the retarded // for i am young / i am forever // eternal adolescent / they look after me / they worry i'll hear the call of the mountain she- devil / like so

many before me / want me quiet by their side // a mcguffin shining in my hands / shining the promise of the day / for it is today / every year / it is today that i'm able to die //// when i feel my members freezing / like so many before me / when i take place among the chosen ones / among their iced muscles and tendons / contorted freckles of their skin / fastened in carnal embrace / a humming swarm / with the crackling noise of successive congealing / never-endingly i am in weaning //// meanwhile the train passengers climax indefinitely // hypothermia for an ultimate hallucination //

Switzerland has legislatively permitted assisted suicide since 1942. A Dignitas clinic near Zürich organizes the pentobarbital coma and death-sleeping mode. 25% of teenager suicides are committed contradictorily in winter time, in the snow, via hypothermia.

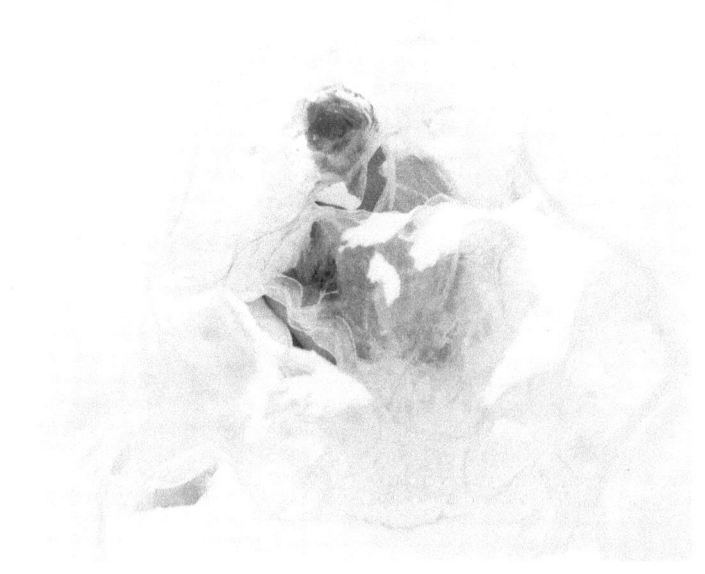

Critical Apparatuses
Bart Lootsma

Something makes people want to walk, ride or climb to the moun-
taintops — how dangerous an undertaking this may be because of
conditions of terrain and weather. It is something completely
irrational. Some have themselves brought to the tops of mountains with trains, cable cars and even helicopters. It is often
thought that this is to appreciate a sublime, untameable nature, since it has been already the theme of many a sublime Ro-
mantic painting or poem. But in fact most Alpine mountain tops
are as artificial as a Dutch polder, not just with the crosses
on top, but with mines dug underneath, avalanche protection,
restaurants, hotels, ski slopes, ski lifts, half-pipes for
snowboarders, artificial lakes to produce artificial snow, a
view of the urbanized valley below, and in summer, cows not
for the production of milk and meat but for maintenance. All
of this is realized only to enable people dressed in special
clothes, helmets and harnesses, to throw themselves down again
literally as soon as they have arrived on top, using sleighs,
skis, snowboards or specially designed and high-tech so-called
freeride mountain bikes. They hardly have a choice. It has to
go fast. Even the sky is filled with gliders and paragliders,
enjoying the turbulence along the slopes. An aspect of dan-
ger, and at least a flirtation with a latent death wish should
be involved to feel alive, as a faint memory of older myths.
"Everywhere it is machines — real ones, not figurative ones: machines driving other machines, machines being driven by other
machines, with all the necessary couplings and connections,"
Deleuze and Guattari write, and between the different machines
there are just couplings and passages, "functioning smoothly
at times, at other times it fits and starts"(1). The Alps are
one big Bachelor Machine, a perpetual carrousel that turns the
love for nature into a death mechanism.

Innsbruck, the city where I live, is one of the innovation cen-
tres of Alpine sports. The 'shadows' of Bruno Taut and his Alpine Architecture are haunting the stations for the funicular
railway up to the Hungerburg as glass memories of the shapes
that remain after an ice storm. From the Hungerburg a cable
car takes people further up to the North Park with the Seegrube
and the Hafelekar, just left of which we find a mountain peak
called Frau Hitt. According to different sagas, Frau Hitt once
was a woman, a giant queen. About why she turned to stone the
stories differ but the best-known version tells that she was
so stingy, that when a beggar asked for some food, she gave him

a stone instead. So the beggar cursed her, turning Frau Hitt and her horse into stone and leaving her in the place where we can still find her today. In winter she is dressed in snow; in spring she unveils herself to become the unreachable piece of stone she is in summer, alternatively attracting and repelling us. All in all, we can see the landscape of the Nordkette in Innsbruck as a complex ecosystem, which is defined by man and nature in equal parts. It includes the social, the economical and even the incorporeal and invisible systems of language: myths, sagas and fairy tales.

It is no different with the landscape of La Diavolezza, a mountain and skiing area near Pontresina in the Swiss Alps, named after a beautiful fairy-queen who allegedly seduced young huntsmen who saw her bathing in Lej Nair, a frozen lake at the summit of the Bernina Pass. The huntsmen who followed her disappeared mysteriously and somehow one must expect they were frozen to death. Freezing to death is a known method for suicide, described among others in Jack London's "To Build a Fire": " … Well, he was bound to freeze anyway, and he might as well take it decently. With this new-found peace of mind came the first glimmerings of drowsiness. A good idea, he thought, to sleep off to death. It was like taking an anaesthetic. Freezing was not so bad as people thought. There were lots worse ways to die … Then the man drowsed off into what seemed to him the most comfortable and satisfying sleep he had ever known."(2) Suicide is an issue in Switzerland, as suicide assistance is legal there as long as it does not bring profit. The Swiss Dignitas organization legally assists people who want to terminate their own lives albeit not by freezing to death. For the she-devil haunting Lej Nar, the freezing of the huntsmen was not enough though, and she only left the region when the whole mountain was frozen and covered with a glacier.

Other myths, sagas, fairy tales and literary narratives surround the la Diavolezza area. Thomas Mann's sanatoriums in *Tristan* and *The Magic Mountain* might have been situated here, only accessible by a forgotten branch of the Rhaetian Railway, somewhere high up in the mountains. Paul Scheerbart saw them as logical predecessors of an architecture made entirely out of glass, because they lit the Alps. As such, they were the predecessors of Bruno Taut's radiating Alpine Architektur, which would crown the mountain tops like an artificial Alpen-

glühen(3). His protagonists thought they might be healed from
tuberculosis here, in the time before penicillin was discov-
ered. Most of them died, of course.

Who would be better chosen than New-Territories/François Roche,
Camille Lacadee with their friend Pierre Huyghe to explore this
place? Their work — architecture, installations, situations,
films, props — is characterized by a mixture of the archaic and
science fiction, moving between myth-making and 'Pataphysics;
schizo-analysis and paranoia. For New Territories, architecture is not just a pragmatic solution for a problem. It is in
the extended pragmatism of a specific situation, that its identity and meaning is produced, as a hyper-localism, as Roche
calls it, a specific haecceity, an ultimate thisness, a biopsy
of a biotope. This biotope is a part not just of a "deep" or
"shallow ecology", but of something like Deleuze's flat ecolog-
ics, which opens up the "philosophical subject" to the realm of
nonhuman machines, affects, haecceities and what Maturana/Va-
rela call "structural couplings" (4); or Guattari's ecosophy,
which sees ecology as a complex phenomenon which incorporates
human subjectivity, the environment, and social relations(5).

New-Territories produces critical apparatuses in the double
meaning of the word. They construct machines that try to reveal disturbances in the systems we are caught up in: misun-
derstandings, bugs, aberrations, perversions, stutterings. By
doing so they also produce critical apparatuses in the sense
of footnotes: the critical and primary source material that
accompanies an edition of a text. François Roche (whose texts
sometimes produce almost the same quantity of footnotes as
the texts are long, by the way) writes that "machines also
simultaneously produce artefacts, assemblages, multiplicity
and desires and infiltrate the 'raison d'être' of our own body
and mind in the relationship to our own biotopes"(6). Thus the
props and McGuffins (7) New Territories make, like the frozen
bodies and their miniatures for La Diavolezza, may trigger
complex and unpredictable events, which in the end may only
exist in our memory or imagination but reveal something about
our complex and ambivalent relation to the Alps.

69

Footnotes

(1) Gilles Deleuze and Félix Guattari, Anti-Oedipus; Capitalism and Schizophrenia, Penguin Books, London, 2009, p. 1.

(2) Jack London, "To Build a Fire," in: Jack London, "Stories of the North:, The World of Jack London," http://www.jacklondons.net/buildafire.html.

(3) Paul Scheerbart, Glasarchitektur & Glashausbriefe, Verlag Klaus G. Renner, , München, 1986, pp. 57; Bruno Taut, "Alpine Architektur," in: Matthias Schirren and, Bruno Taut, "Alpine Architektur, Eine Utopie - A Utopia," Prestel, München/Berlin/London/New York, 2004, pp. 27-115.

(4) Bernd Herzogenrath, "Nature/Geophilosophy/Machinics/Ecosophy," in: Bernd Herzogenrath, "Deleuze/Guattari & Ecology," Palgrave MacmMillan, Houndmills, Basingstoke/New York, 2009, pp. 11-12.

(5) Félix Guattari, "The Three Ecologies," Continuum Impacts, London/ New York, 2008.

(6) François Roche, "Alchimis(t/r/ick)-machines)," Log 22, Spring/Summer 2011, http://www.anycorp.com/log/22.

(7) In fiction, a McGuffin is a plot device in the form of some goal, desired object, or other motivator that the protagonist pursues, often with little or no narrative explanation. The specific nature of a MacGuffin is unimportant to the overall plot. See http://en.wikipedia.org/ wiki/MacGuffin.

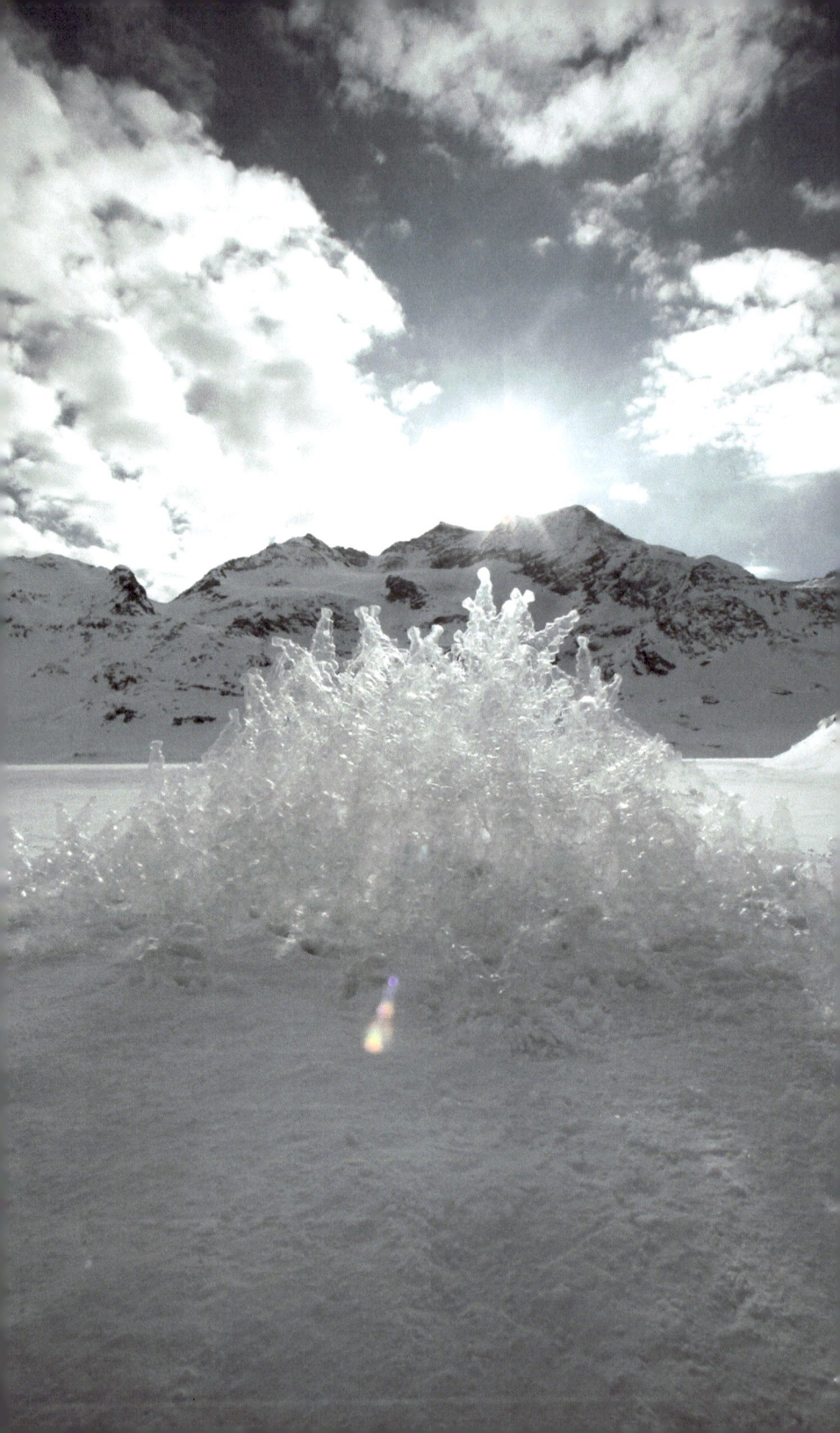

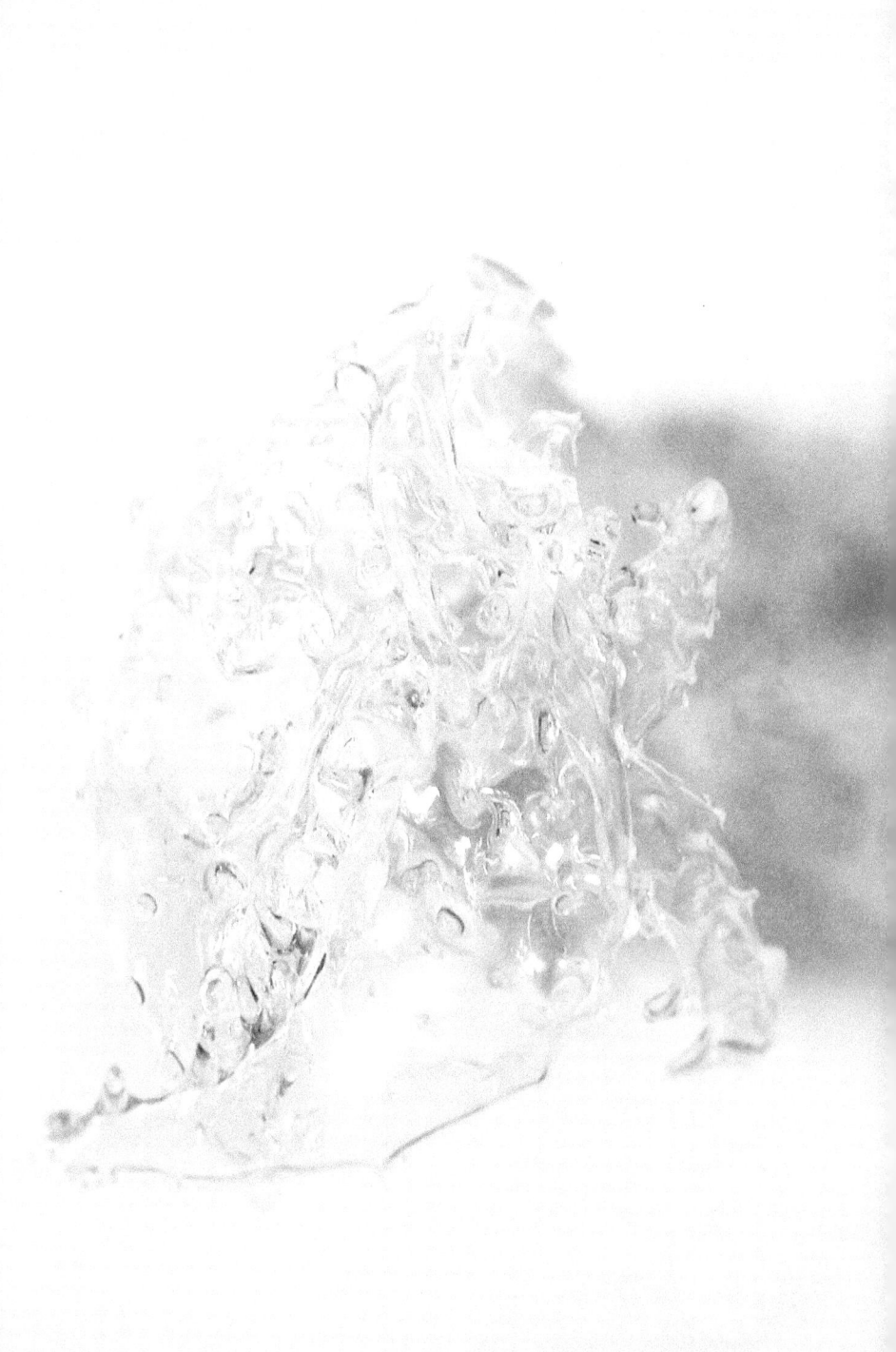

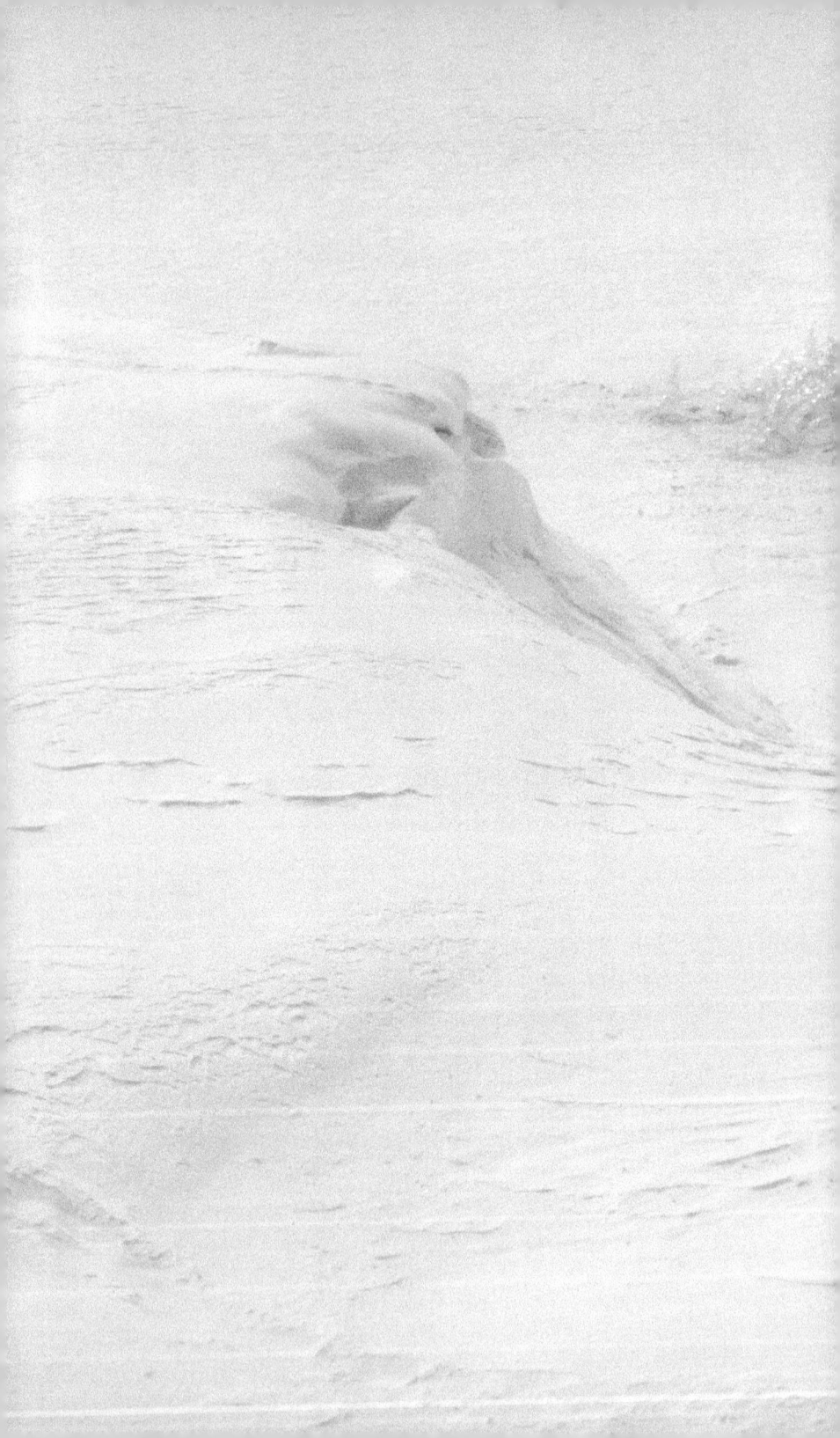

name:	Naχos (terra īnsōla)
year:	2013
location:	Crete, Greece
pathology:	dissociative identity disorder
prop:	500 pee-cured ceramic extrusions \ steel structure \\ future ruin status
duration:	04:07
pitch:	Daedalus artefact's | artefact |

/ the bastard dumped me there / alone on naχos / disembarked / that mas-macho gone with my sister / ah / theseus-testosterone / killer of my half-monster-half-brother // betrayal is your nature / am i so naïve / what now / celebration of food and wine / dionysius the alcoholic / turning me into a multi-procreative uterus // trapped in suspended time / daedalus you could have been a little more thought- through / wooden cow trick for my mother-copulation / minotaur p r o c r e a t i o n / tortuous labyrinth / last bath of minos / the love thread spell / the melting wax-wings // you are the first very architect / composing your mistake-failure with another one and so on //// now i escape from inside / embrace a topological inversion / an infinite fortressless animism / releasing me / congealing me in / my state of limbo-libido / and i pee merrily on my past and my future /

According to Lyotard, every political economy is libidinal: that intensity has no equivalent in currency does not rid the circuits of capital of the force of libidinal investment. Intensive "exchanges" are ignorant of the constitutive negation of both political economy and natural theology since the libido invests unconditionally.

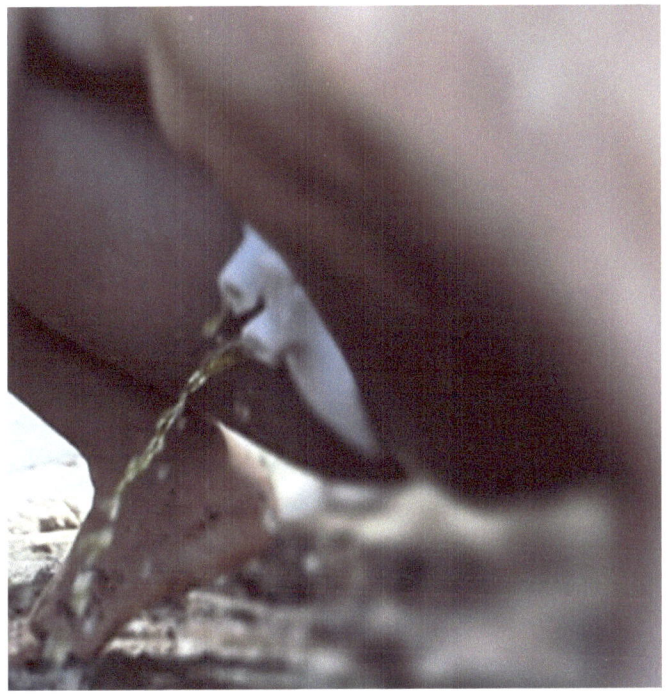

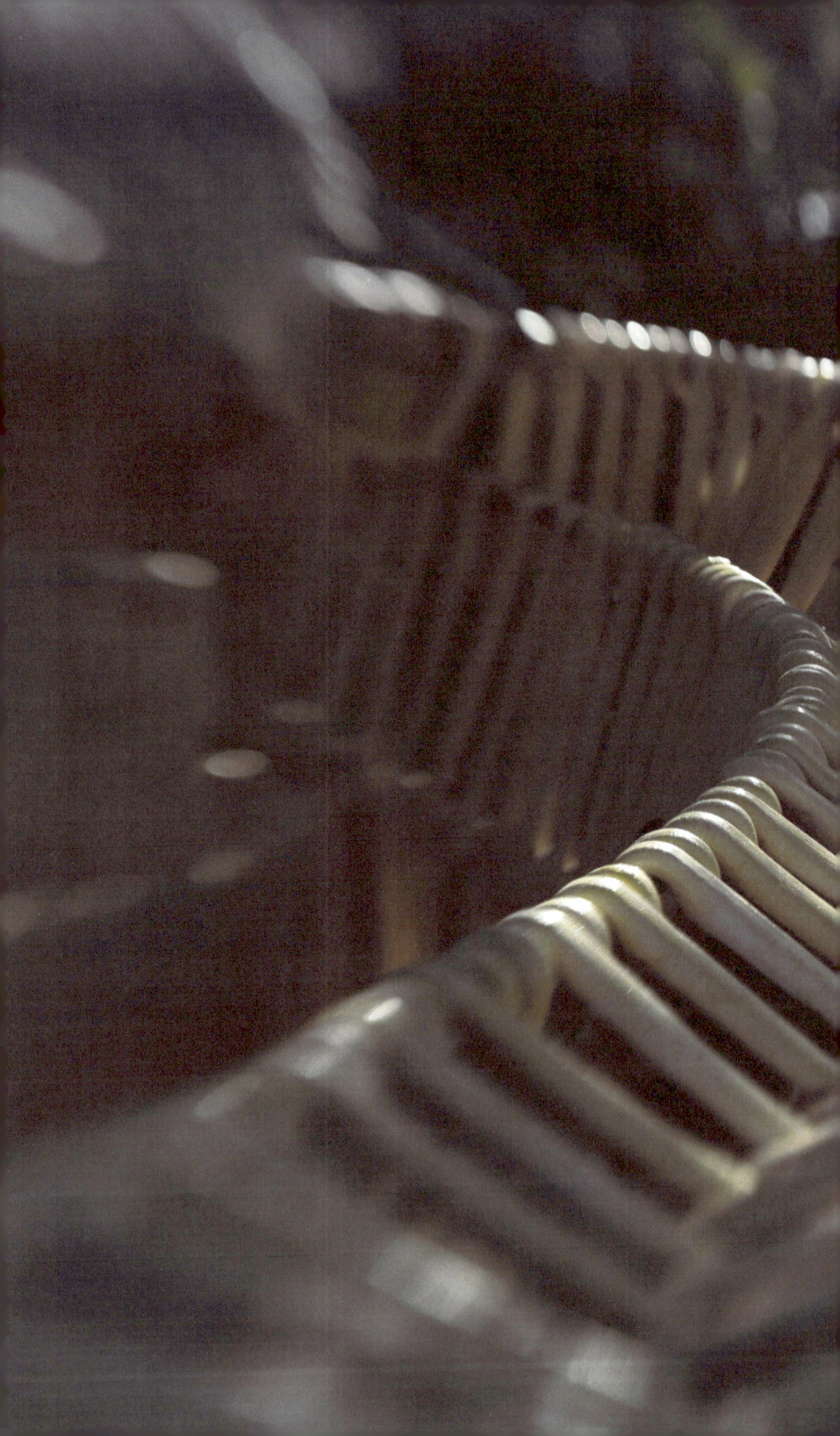

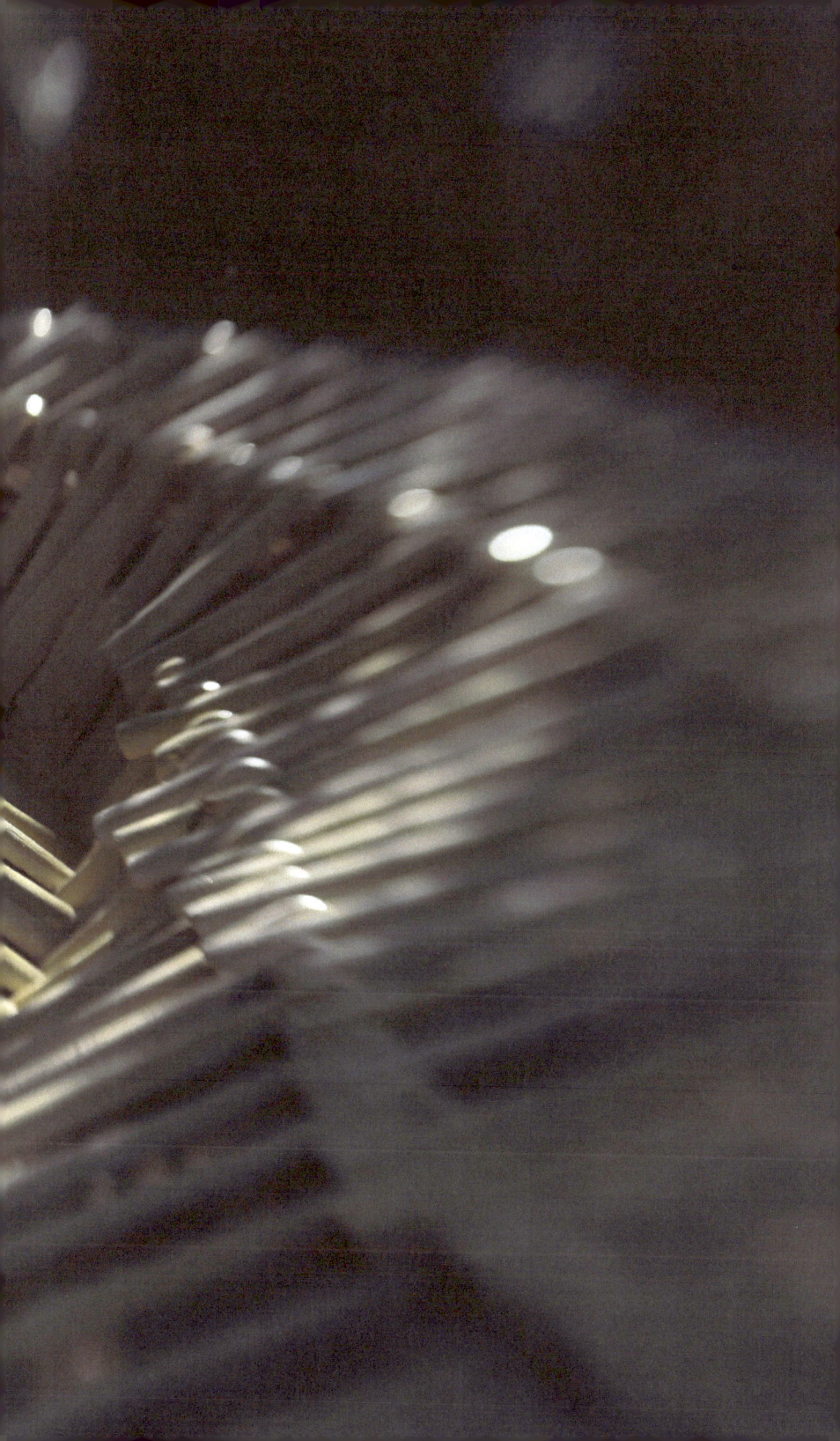

name:	Timidity Symptom
year:	june 2013-april 2014
location:	Bangkok, Thailand
pathology:	erethism erotica mercurialis
prop:	15000 thermoformed plastic components \ allelopathic chemical agents \ steel & concrete structure \\ aborted
duration:	03:09
pitch:	shyness through | the battlefield |

/ a ghostly emergence in the jungle / trismegistus 32 m high / sombre reverb shadows negotiating the right distance / between flirtation and repulsion / feeding and fighting // a silent war // between proto and crypto / computational conflict in the negative void of a tropical forest / do not touch me // reciprocally // pheromonal timidity / unstable equilibrium / no status quo / in this latent conflict / with power without accomplishment / a toxic void / allelopathic chemistry / crown shyness tension /

Allelopathy (also called 'crown shyness'), etymologically, "to suffer from each other," is the active or passive effect of chemicals released into the environment influencing the growth, survival and reproduction of other organisms.

Pp. 90-91, point cloud model from a 3D laser scanning of the jungle (extract).

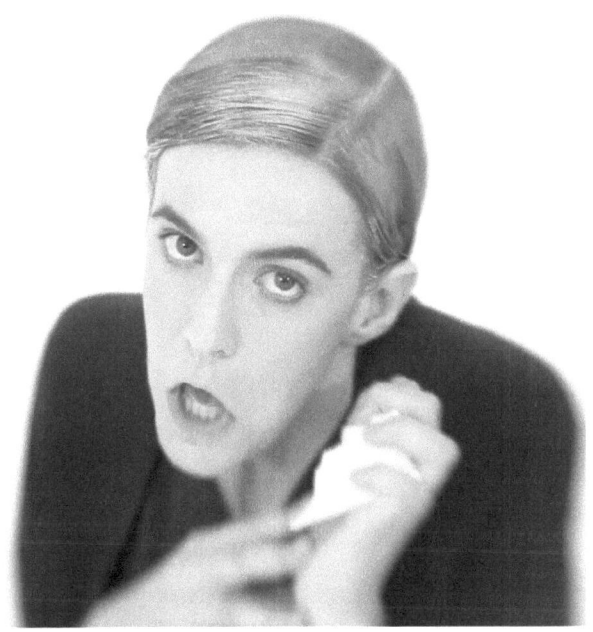

Allelopathy Anthropophobia
/ erethism erotica mercurialis
Camille Lacadee

```
\ / /
(*)~-------------------------------------------------------
------------------------
 Pitch for a feature film set in Timidity projects for Mr. O, in
2015 BKK, by New-Territories [eɪf/bʌt/c] architects.
---
 Code re-interpreted from Moritz Kassner & William Patera
python code for Pupil — eye-tracking platform.
---
 Script guided by 2 voices: the code used with the pupil &
eardrum recording devices, and the inner monologue of the
hero. A third, psychotic interference of the psyche, regularly
surfaces.
-------------------------------------------------------------
---------------------~(*)
\ / /
```

INT.-EXT. FOLIAGE - BANGKOK - SUNSET - 2015

```
import sys,os
import cv2 as cv
import numpy as np
import cProfile
import time
```

Sounds of birds … and insects … cicadas … faraway sounds of
monkeys, voices nearby, sounds of glasses, laughter, and … my
name …

```
def main():
    save_video = False
```

Slowly coming out of the mist… mind mist … grey … and all
around … stains … undulations … … leaves … slowly undulating
leaves … I focus … texture … undulations of the texture … a
rhythm… in grey translucence … … some branches behind, further
away … different … black … black
Open again … clearer … people … a lot of people … filling
the frame …... drinking … eating finger food … undulating …
smartly chatting … touching delicately … or gesticulating … not
attached to each other … representation … vague connections …
I see …
```
    try:
```

```
        data_folder = sys.argv[1]
    except:
        print "You did not supply a datafolder when you called
this script. \
            \nI will use the path hardcoded into the script
instead."
        data_folder = "/Users/Timidity/Desktop/002"

    if not os.path.isdir(data_folder):
        raise Exception("Please supply a layer of memories")
```

I hear … indistinctly … glasses choked … small talks, laughers
… high pitch voices … 'really?' absolutely fabulous!' ' ah
yes … ? and have you had the chance to visit yet? …' leaves
rustling … 'no no … only from rumours …' ' he is so … hmm …
shy … you know …' ' but tonight I have hope … I have hope …'
'oh there he is! …'

```
     # when we first see the word 'shy' it should appear as a
scandal
    video_path = data_folder + "/world.avi"
    timestamps_path = data_folder + "/timestamps.npy"
    gaze_positions_path = data_folder + "/gaze_positions.npy"
    record_path = data_folder + "/world_viz.avi"
```

Now I am the bacteria on your lip

```
    cap = cv.VideoCapture(video_path)
    gaze_list = list(np.load(gaze_positions_path))
    timestamps = list(np.load(timestamps_path))
   # gaze_list: gaze x | gaze y | pupil x | pupil y | timestamp
   # timestamps timestamp
```

A BOURGEOISE
 'Mr O'! Mr O … !'
'My … what a house you have! I first took it for the museum…
where is it? Let me introduce you to my husband … an artist as
well … would love to see your collection … your fantasies …
I have heard too much about it … How do we get there? Will you
show us? tonight … ?'

```
     # this takes the timestamps list and makes a list
     # with the length of the number of recorded frames.
      # Each slot contains a list that will have 0, 1 or more
associated gaze positions.
    positions_by_frame = [[] for i in timestamps]
```

Zoom in … lips … drinking … lipstick on the glass … red stripes
… uneven … irregular … She smiles … looks at me … insistence …
look down … zoom out … mist …

```
    no_frames = len(timestamps)
    frame_idx = 0
    data_point = gaze_list.pop(0)
    gaze_point = data_point[:2]
    gaze_timestamp = data_point[4]
```

Open again … slowly … still down … dark wood from the tropics
… feet … high heels … legs … bare

```
    while gaze_list:
        # if the current gaze point is before the mean of the
current world frame timestamp and the next worldframe timestamp
            if gaze_timestamp <= (timestamps[frame_
idx]+timestamps[frame_idx+1])/2.:
            positions_by_frame[frame_idx].append({'x': gaze_
point[0],'y':gaze_point[1], 'timestamp':gaze_timestamp})
            data_point = gaze_list.pop(0)
            gaze_point = data_point[:2]
            gaze_timestamp = data_point[4]
```

Too long … they will notice … look up … slowly … freeze … give
me a moment

```
        else:
            if frame_idx >= no_frames-2:
                break
            frame_idx+=1

    status, img = cap.read()
    prevgray = cv.cvtColor(img, cv.COLOR_BGR2GRAY)
    height, width = img.shape[0:2]
    frame = 0
    past_gaze = []
    t = time.time()
```

Now I am the termite under your skin

```
    fps = cap.get(5)
    wait = int((1./fps)*1000)
```

Look up … leaves … shading … getting darker … greyer … shades
of the leaves above my head suddenly go from light grey to dark
… deep dark … a passing cloud … I loose visual connection to
the garden

```
    if save_video:
```

```
#FFV1 -- good speed lossless big file
#DIVX -- good speed good compression medium file
        writer  =  cv.VideoWriter(record_path,  cv.cv.CV_
FOURCC(*'DIVX'), fps, (img.shape[1], img.shape[0]))
```

Turn around … behind the glass accordion … on my left … a silhouette … approaching … very smart … thin … quite small … discreet

```
    while status and frame < no_frames:
        nt = time.time()
        # print nt-t
        t = nt
        # apply optical flow displacement to previous gaze
```

'Excuse me'

```
        if past_gaze:
            gray = cv.cvtColor(img, cv.COLOR_BGR2GRAY)
            prevPts = np.array(past_gaze,dtype=np.float32)
            nextPts = prevPts.copy()
        nextPts, status, err = cv.calcOpticalFlowPyrLK(prevgray,
gray,prevPts,nextPts)
            prevgray = gray
```

INT. RCC GROTTO - CIVIL TWILLIGHT

Faster … down … down … don't stop … follow him … turn here … there … don't stop … don't talk … pretend you're in a hurry
```
            past_gaze = list(nextPts)

            #constrain gaze positions to
```

Strata … rough … skin … torn … passing by … small scrapes … unnoticeable … undramatic … lame …
Feet on the ground … grass in between slabs … traces of guests

```
            c_gaze = []
            for x,y in past_gaze:
                if x >0 and x<width and y >0 and y <height:
                    c_gaze.append([x,y])
            past_gaze = c_gaze
```

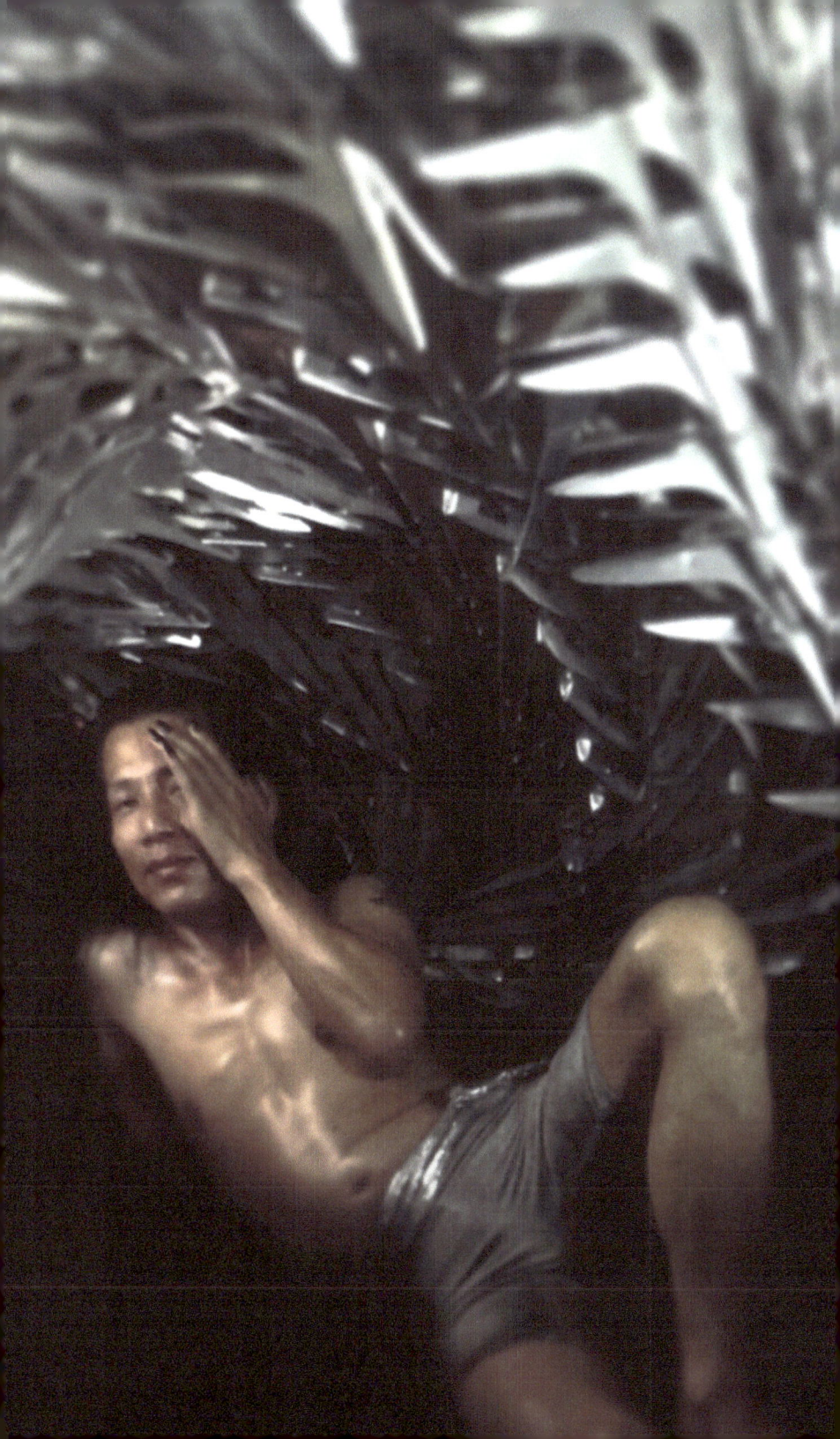

INT.-EXT. CANOPY - NAUTICAL TWILLIGHT

Now a clearing … a void in the foliage … …
Now a jungle … ferns … stronger noise of insects …
Dark light … dark green of the night continuously falling … …
dilatation
```
        #load and map current gaze positions and append to the
past_gaze list
        current_gaze = positions_by_frame[frame]
        for gaze_point in current_gaze:
            dilatation = mydriasis ((gaze_point['x'], gaze_
point['y']), 2, max)
```

I follow … I remember … super-imposition of images … I foresee
… in between the trees … wild tiny prisoners
```
        for gaze_point in current_gaze:
         x,y = denormalize((gaze_point['x'], gaze_point['y']),
width, height)
            if x >0 and x<width and y >0 and y <height:
                past_gaze.append([x,y])

        vap = 20 #Visual_Attention_Span
        window_string = "the last %i frames of visual attention"
%vap
        overlay = np.zeros(img.shape,dtype=img.dtype)

        # remove everything but the last "vap" number of gaze
positions from the list of past_gazes
        for x in xrange(len(past_gaze)-vap):
            past_gaze.pop(0)
```
Now I am a butterfly in your thoughts

```
           # draw recent gaze positions as white spots on an
overlay image.
        for gaze_point in past_gaze[::-1]:
            cv.circle(overlay,(int(gaze_point[0]),int(gaze_
point[1])), int(vap*2), (255, 255, 255), int(vap*6))
```

Keep on… don't stop … follow the silhouette through your own
garden
```
            vap -=.9 # less recent gaze points are smaller
            vap = max(1,vap)
```

```
        #render the area of visual attention as sharp sights
on blurred visions
```

Animals screams … wild … serene … of life and death … the
gibbons, the insects … and everything else …
Each instant dying and resurrecting

```
        blurred = cv.blur(img,(21,21))
        # desaturate the image
        # blurred = cv.cvtColor(blurred,cv.COLOR_BGR2GRAY)
        # blurred = cv.cvtColor(blurred,cv.COLOR_GRAY2BGR)
        blurred *=.8
```

To become them

```
        # multiply this overlay with the img (white spot = 1,
black background = 0)
        # img = cv.multiply(img,overlay/255)
        mask = (overlay==255)
        blurred[mask] = img[mask]
        cv.imshow(window_string, blurred)
        if save_video:
            writer.write(blurred)
```

When … beneath the branches and the screams … a deformation …
there's a pause … all slowing down … until I am in front

INT. CANOPY - ASTRONOMICAL TWILLIGHT

There was no boundary between where I came from and where I am
now … perhaps just a change in light … no pressure …

```
        status, img = cap.read()
        frame += 1
        ch = cv.waitKey(wait)
        if ch == 27:
            break
```

Muffled sounds … a mass of bodies … immobile … on top of each
other … assembled … everywhere …

```
def denormalize(pos, width, height, flip_y=True):
```

Extreme close-up … closer … touching … lightly … see through
them … slow motion … my hand on a chest … grab the hair … black

```
    """
    denormalize and return as free
```

\"""

INT. WHITE BOUNDARYLESS - DUSK

Open again … white void … intense light … hurting … the glare
… close eyelid … signs … vibrations … too strong … … no sound

```
    x = pos[0]
    y = pos[1]
    if flip_y:
```

I lose sight of my guide

```
        y= -y
    x = (x * width / 2.) + (width / 2.)
    y = (y * height / 2.) + (height / 2.)
    return x,y
```

EXT. HOLE - NIGHT

```
def mydriasis(pos, lightIntensity, diameter):
        # to be specified
def dazzle(intensity, color):
        # to be specified
def tears(humidity, blur, pain):
        # to be specified
if __name__ == '__main__':
    main()
```

```
    # code and scenario to be developed
```

INT. CANOPY - DAWN

They come … they enter … I hear them walking up … I hear the
elevator … the gates …
I feel the gaze … the pupils wandering … I am immobile … they
came to get lost … they will become part of it … as well

Now you cannot see me

NOTES ~~(work in progress)~~

- Erethism or erethism mercurialis is a neurological disorder which affects the whole central nervous system, as well as a symptom complex derived from mercury poisoning. This is also sometimes known as the Mad Hatter disease. Historically, this was common among old England felt-hatmakers who used mercury to stabilize the wool in a process called felting, where hair was cut from a pelt of an animal such as a rabbit. The industrial workers were exposed to the mercury vapours, giving rise to the expression "mad as a hatter." Some believe that the character the Mad Hatter in Lewis Carroll's "Alice in Wonderland" is an example of someone suffering from erethism ….
It is commonly characterized through behavioural changes such as irritability, low self-confidence, depression, apathy, shyness and timidity, and in some extreme cases with prolonged exposure to mercury vapours, delirium, personality changes and memory loss occur as a result. People with erethism find it difficult to interact socially with others, with behaviours similar to that of a social phobia.

- Phases = Muscular tension / Blushing / Perspiration / Mouth dryness / Palpitation / Nausea / Restraint / Delirium

- Charles Darwin devoted Chapter 13 of his 1872 The Expression of the Emotions in Man and Animals to complex emotional states including self-attention, shame, shyness, modesty and blushing. He described blushing as "the most peculiar and most human of all expressions."

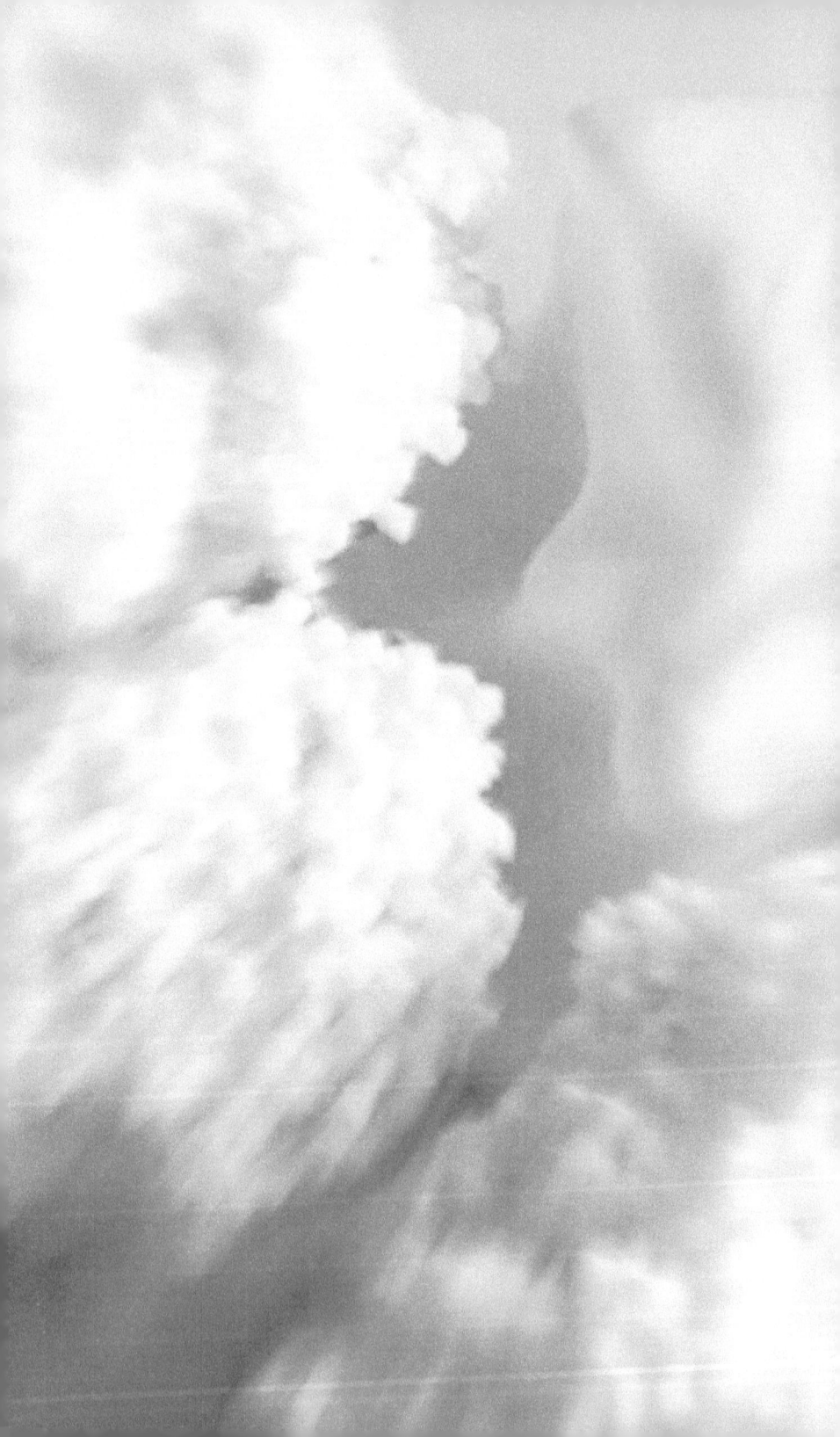

name: emet

year: 2015

location: River City, Bangkok, Thailand

pathology: hutchinson-gilford progeria syndrome

prop: 200 ceramic components \ robotic RSI-perturbation extrusion \\ 2 weeks

duration: 02:16

pitch: Diogenes'| looking-glass |

/ symmetric behaviour / strikethrough life and death / tads and dotards facing their suspicious candour and instinctual obscenity / cruel laughter / sardonic growling // no words / ignorance on the verge of alzheimer's / sneering with borborygmi / gobbling and snoring / slobbering / drooling through  i d e n t i c a l reflections in the mirror / a multitude of janus double-faces // projection / illusion / the escape from those two states of sarcasm / in the darkness of the street / man faces me to get the backlash of his creation / to articulate his 'reason of being' / time-break of god's existence // the perpetuation of the scene of the crime / without hope / pandora's box / and 'you think it's funny' /

Diogenes of Sinope was a Greek philosopher and one of the founders of Cynic philosophy. He maintained that all the artificial growths of society were incompatible with happiness and that morality implies a return to the simplicity of nature: "Humans have complicated every simple gift of the gods." An exile and an outcast, a man with no social identity, Diogenes had nothing but disdain for Plato and his abstract philosophy, he viewed Antisthenes as the true heir to Socrates, and shared his love of virtue and indifference to wealth, together with a disdain for general opinion. Plato once described Diogenes as "a Socrates gone mad."

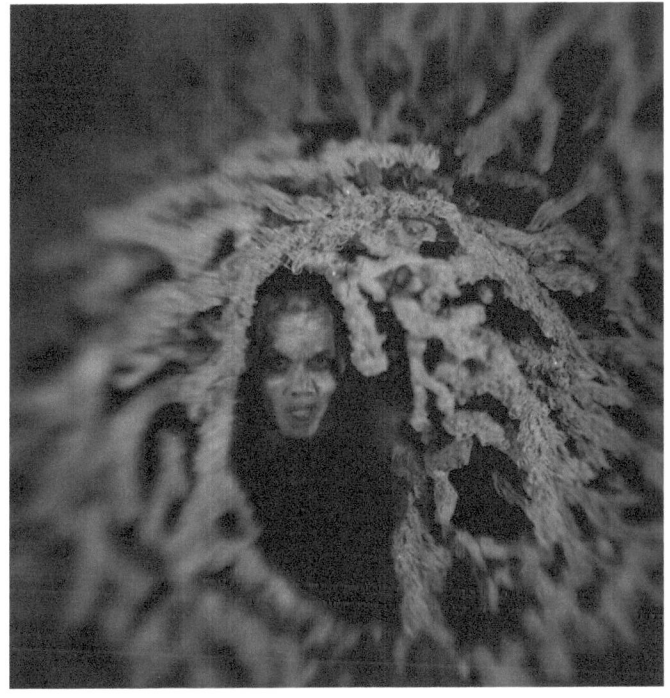

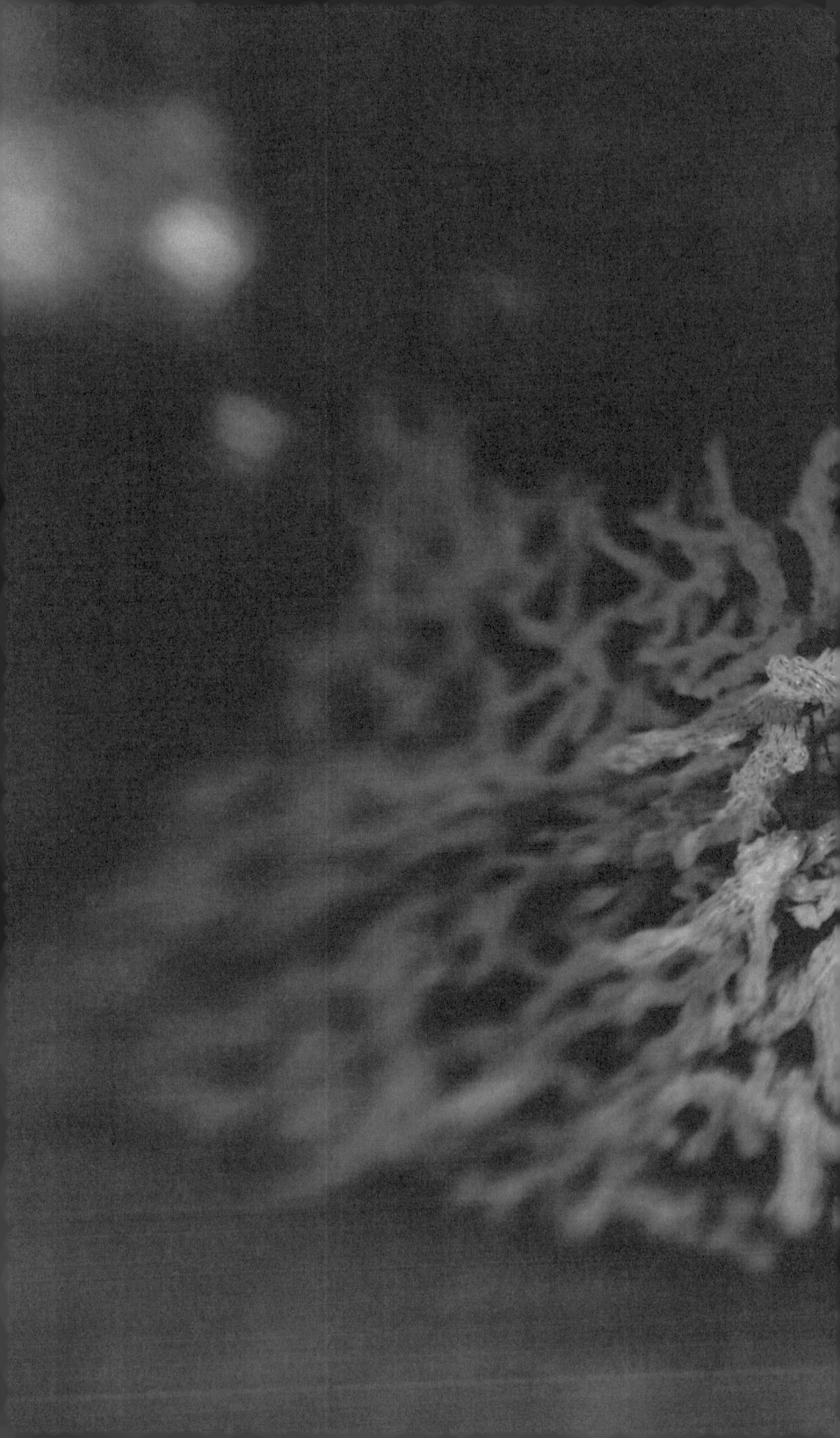

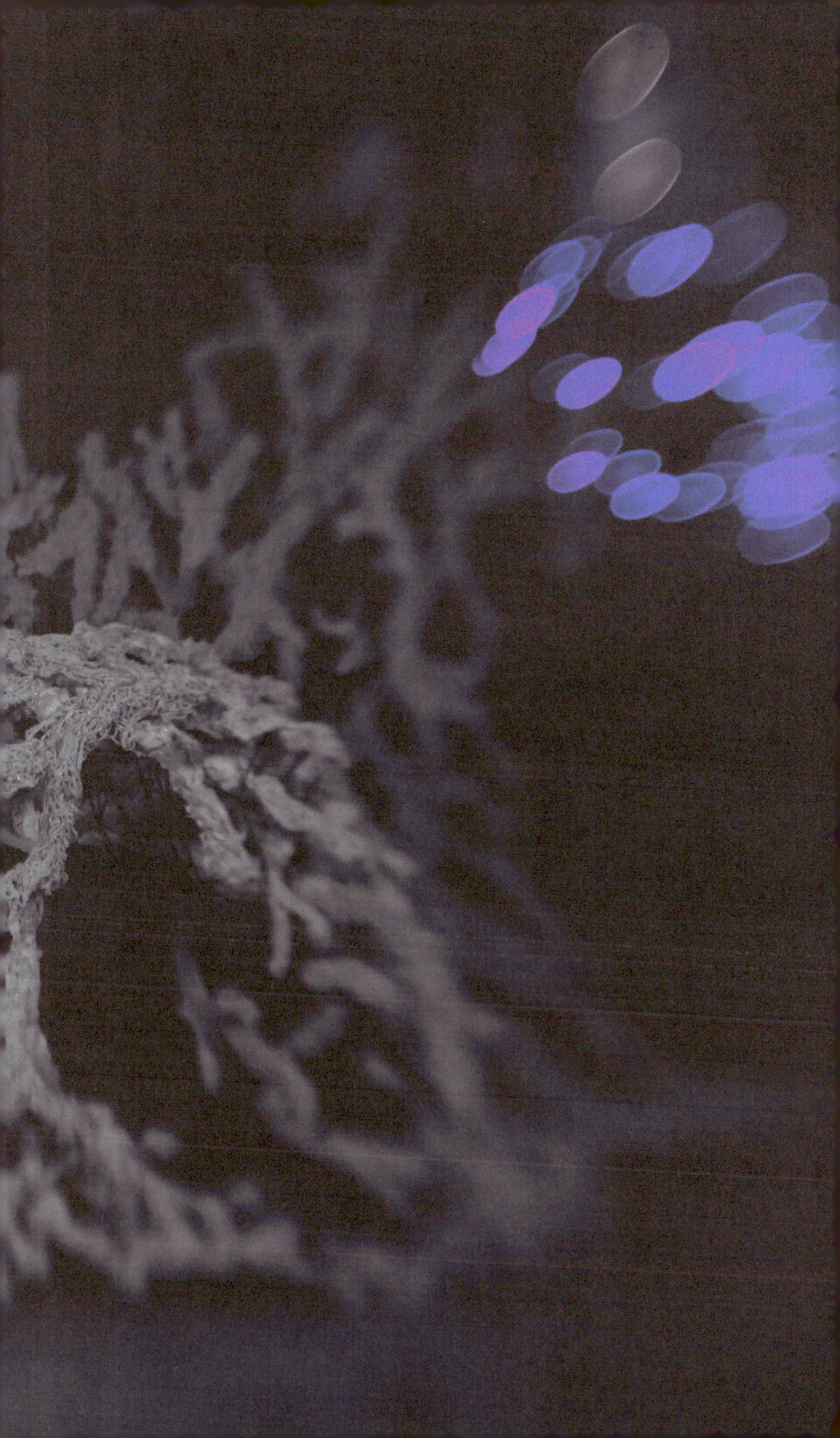

name: Daemon in Venice

year: 2011

location: Khlong Toei, Bangkok, Thailand

pathology: choreomania

prop: 7000 black sandbags
\ 1250 kg of newspaper
\ 30 m3 of sand \ 100 metallic rods
\\ 1 week theater-dance performance

duration: 01:40

pitch: | where | v = √(2gh)

// overflowing discharges in the bottomless sinkhole // absorb // shapeless incontinence briefs // death dance and death figure / way too erotic // body culture body building and guilty desire / flood and sweat and sperm / mixed and soaked up // thomas mann in bangkok  / nauseous chao phraya / emptying and filling / following torricelli // one must sponge it up / soak it up / struggle in the pool's depth / despite all barricades / drowning forecast // i darkness / i sick wind blowing over your land / i cholera / i guilty pleasure and desire / i kill the writer's block / i swamp / aqua alta / water flooding your streets / i a piling-up / a desperate attempt / a macabre dance / i only delay the overflow // but soon enough desire as water breaches human-made obstacles //

In 2011, 30% of Thailand, including Bangkok, was under monsoon waters. The severe flooding was triggered by the landfall of Tropical Storm Nock-ten, and soon spread through the provinces of northern, north-eastern, and central Thailand along the Mekong and Chao Phraya river basins.

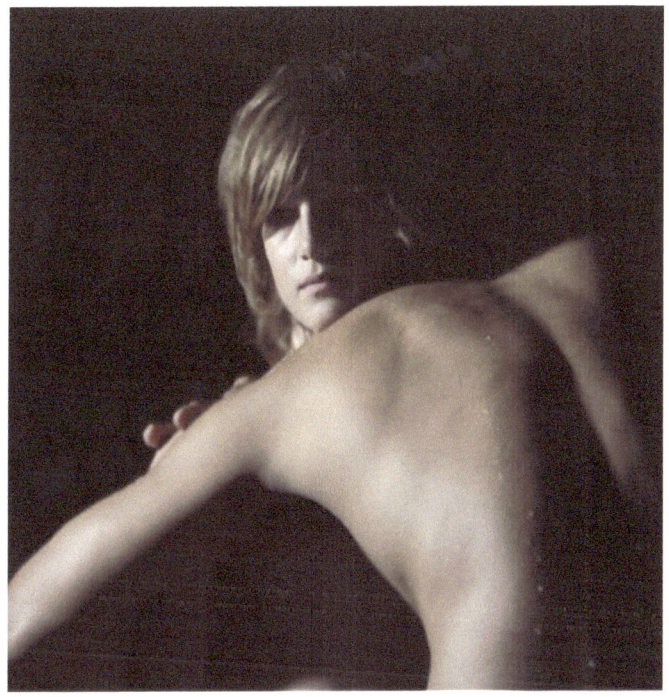

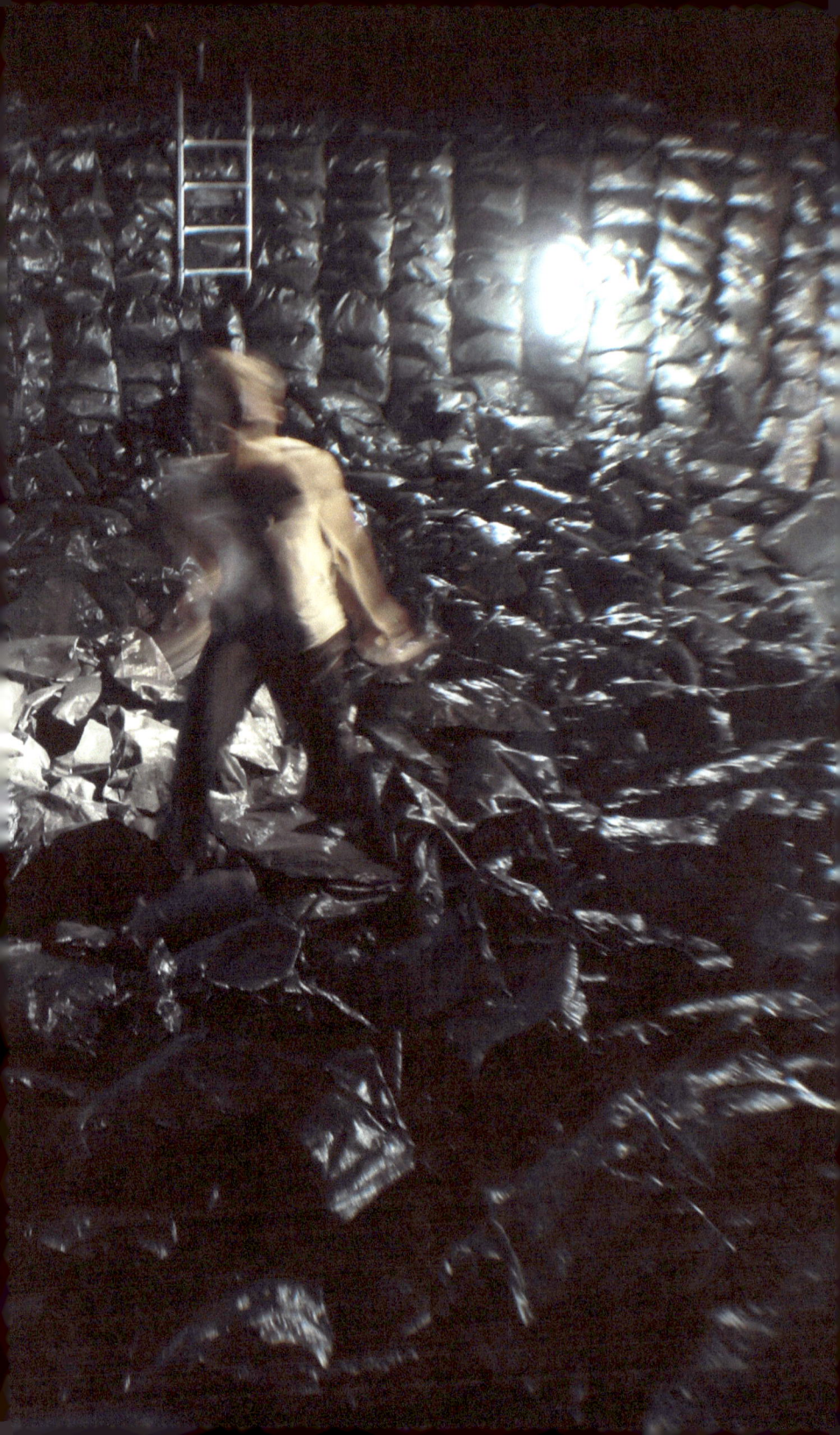

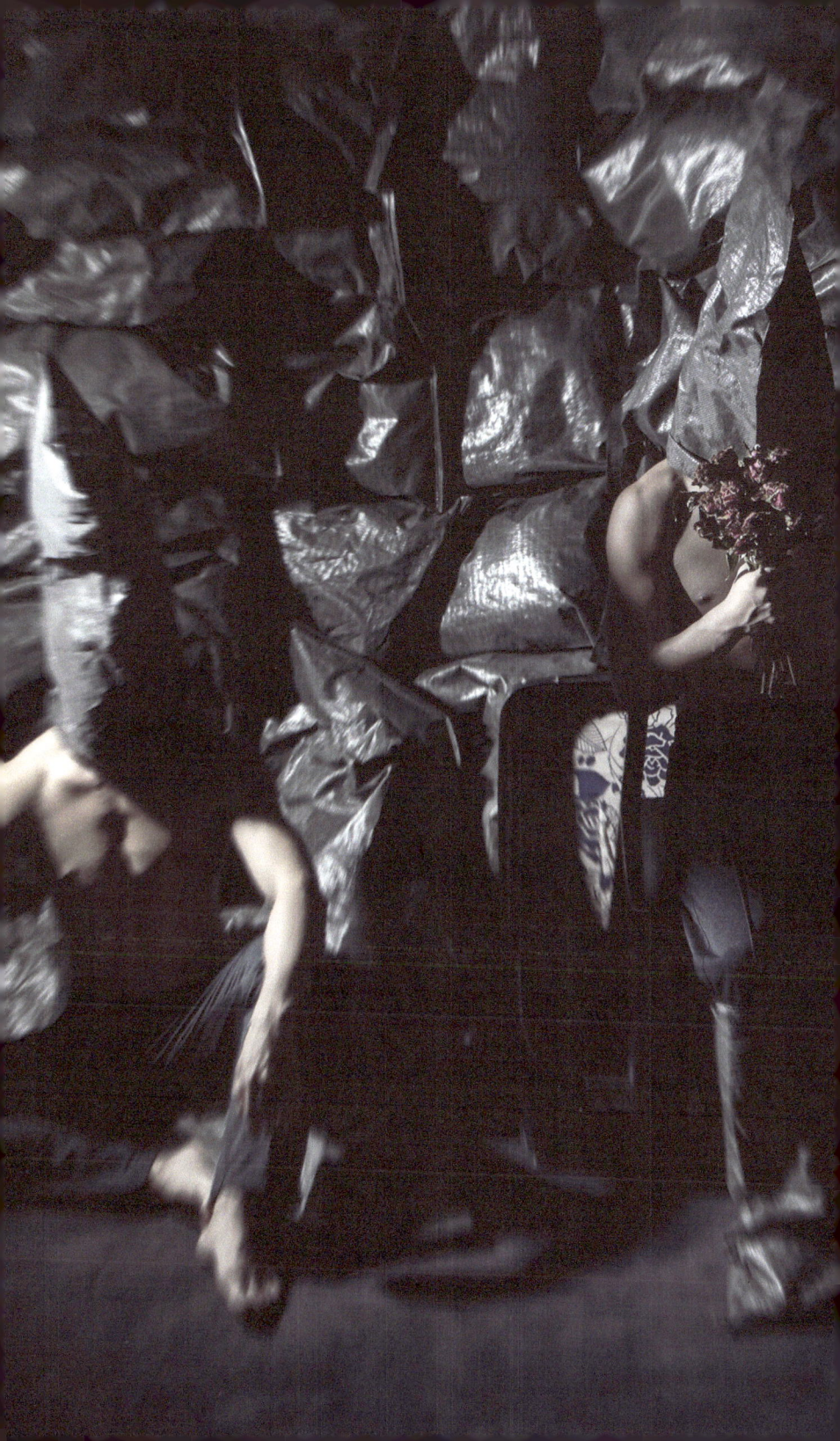

name: Zeitgast

year: 2015

location: Innsbruck, Austria

pathology: subimago stagnation

prop: mix of glucose & ABS
\ filament air spraying
\ silicone \ pump \ pneumatic muscles
\\ 1 night

duration: 05:51

pitch: daily routine | ephemeral suit |
metabolizer

/ i am the unknown ötzi proto-human friend / lost
in a whiteness i could spoil / for a limited time
/ preliminary condition to
rebirth everyday // to make
tomorrow possible  / daily animal
instinct / night psychosis ///
an impulse to make shelter /
diurnal silence / nocturnal
c o n f l i c t s staging my human
schizophrenia // hopefully // call
me sybil / in my multiple echoes
// from larva to nymphas // cycle of repetition / and
exquisite corpses /

"Die Another Day," song by Madonna on the "American Life"
album (2003).

Ötzi the Iceman, visible at the South Tyrol Museum of
Archaeology in Bolzano, is a well-preserved natural mummy of a
Neolithic man who lived around 3300 BCE. His life came to an
abrupt end, and his body has been preserved along with much of
his clothing and possessions intact.

In biology, the imago is the last stage an insect attains during
its metamorphosis, its process of growth and development; it
also is called the imaginal stage, the stage in which the
insect attains maturity. It follows the final ecdysis of the
immature instars. See https://en.wikipedia.org/wiki/Imago.

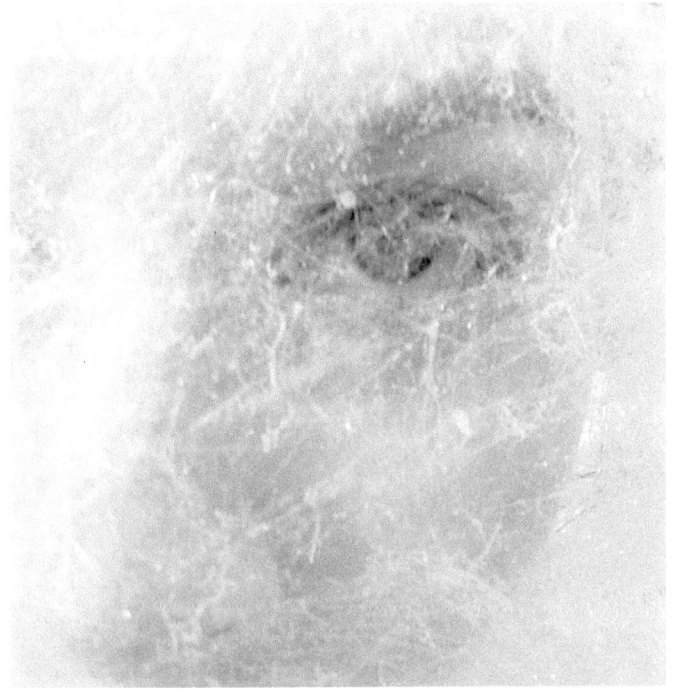

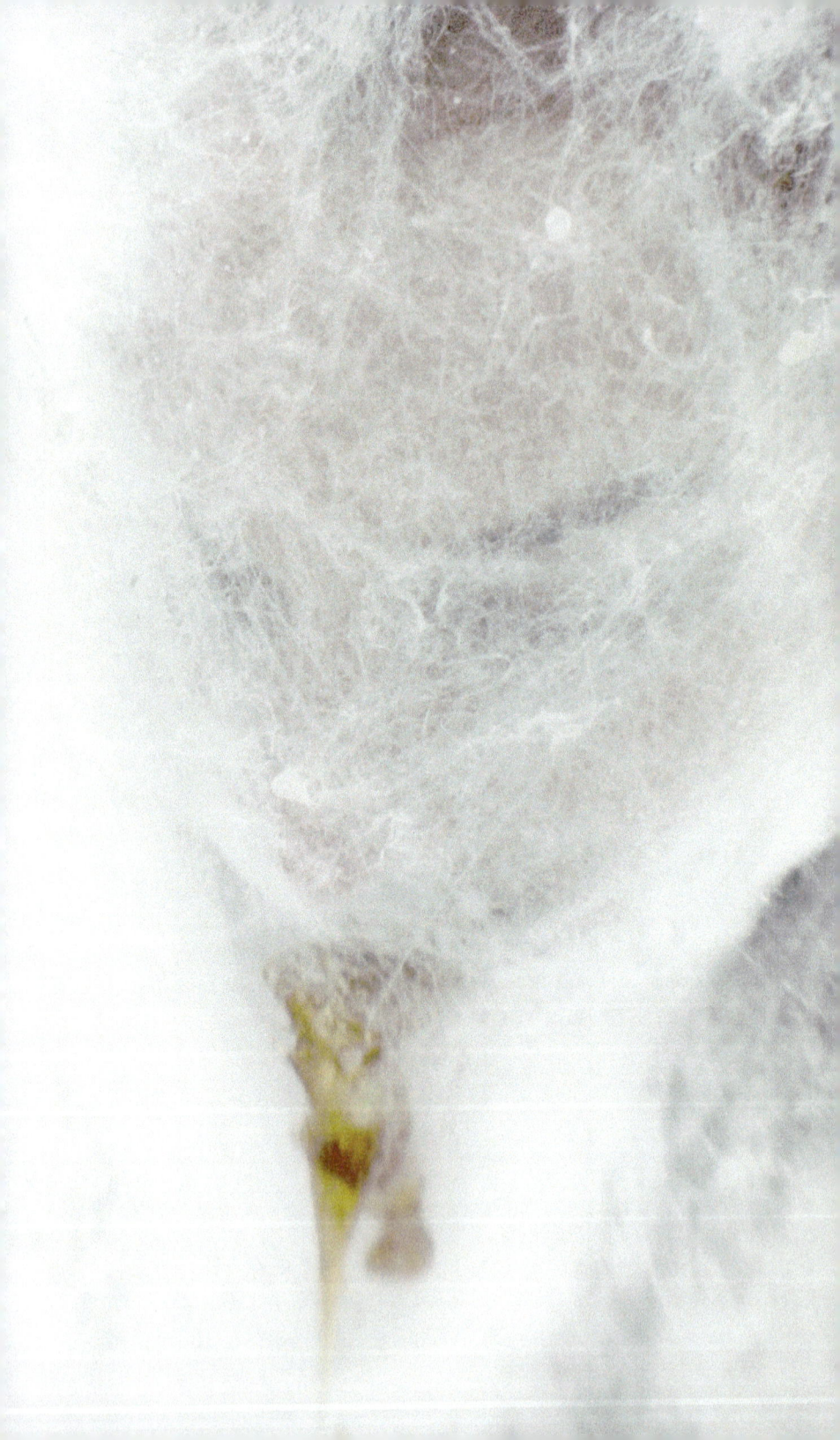

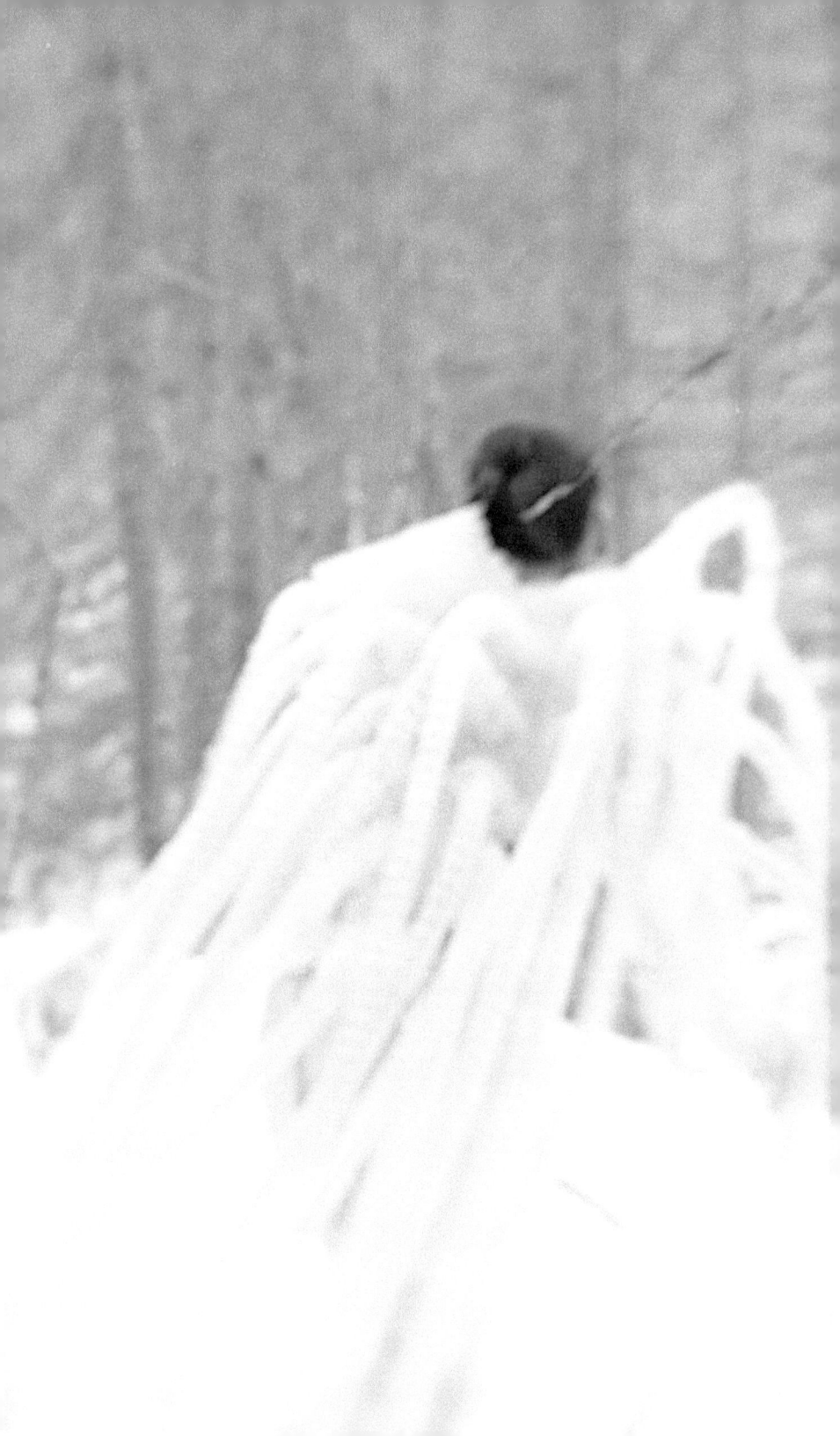

name: Although (in) hapnea

year: 2013

location: Makkasan, Bangkok, Thailand

pathology: metempsychosis

prop: 300 glass-blown aquariums \ nylon strings \\ permanent

duration: 14:30

pitch: entropic anthropocene | self-fishbowl |

// noosphere / i am condemned to exchange chemistry and psychastenia for global energy conservation / second principle of thermodynamic law / metempsychosis to respect the planetary (dis)equilibrium and/or ruptures / vectors // entwined urbanism / unsuspected infrazones / weeping interzone / in additive and subtractive mode // no more dreams of the previous primitive state / no more nature versus artifice // the anthropocene entropy took place / via the planet's complex industrial- anthropological transformation /// we say little gains / little losses / all around / little pains // as modus operandi / a transfer / between species substances voids rules and subjectivities // you say i am the transgression of souls // 3 ecologies / my last words //

In Bourgogne (France), the Vouivre (Wyvern) is a chimera, mi terrestrial mi aquatic, living by the eponymous river.

Forecasting logics are no longer able to predict natural catastrophes, those being generated not by natural spasms but resulting from political, industrial and human conjunctions, … 'Angry' biotopes. Gaïa's furies are countless: Katrina, El Niño, Jeanne, Thomas and Nargis, Xynthia, Ewiniar, Fukujima … a series of devastations and uncertainties that our seismographs cannot prevent. Consequently Guattari's argument is that 'Environmental ecology,' as it exists today, has barely begun to prefigure the generalised ecology (noosphere), the aim of which will be to radically decentre social struggles and ways of coming into one's own psyche …

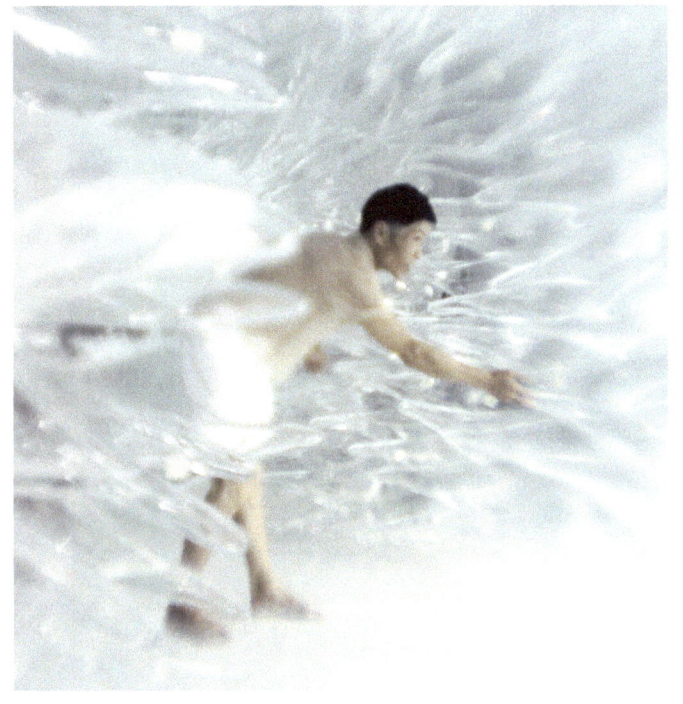

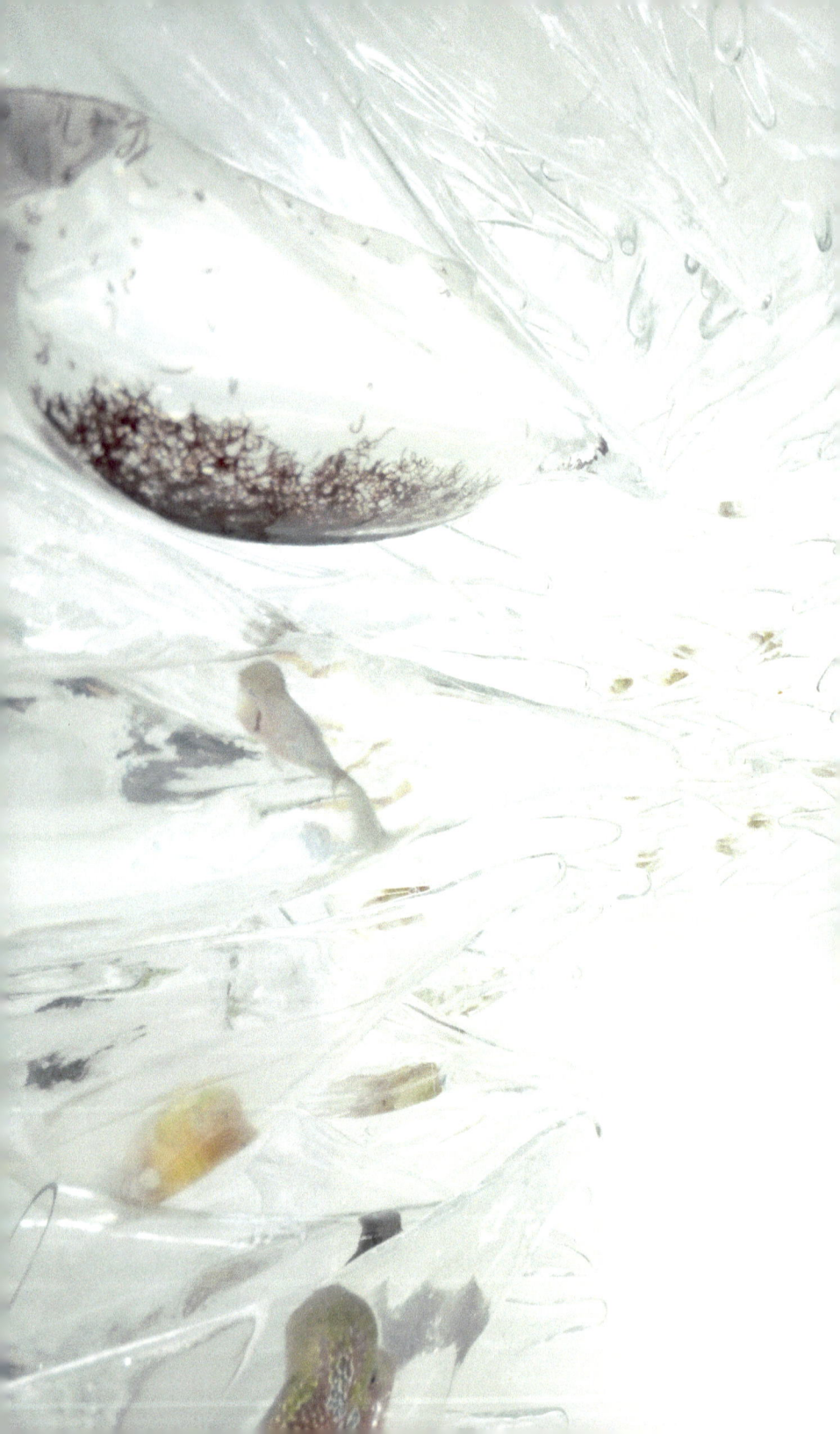

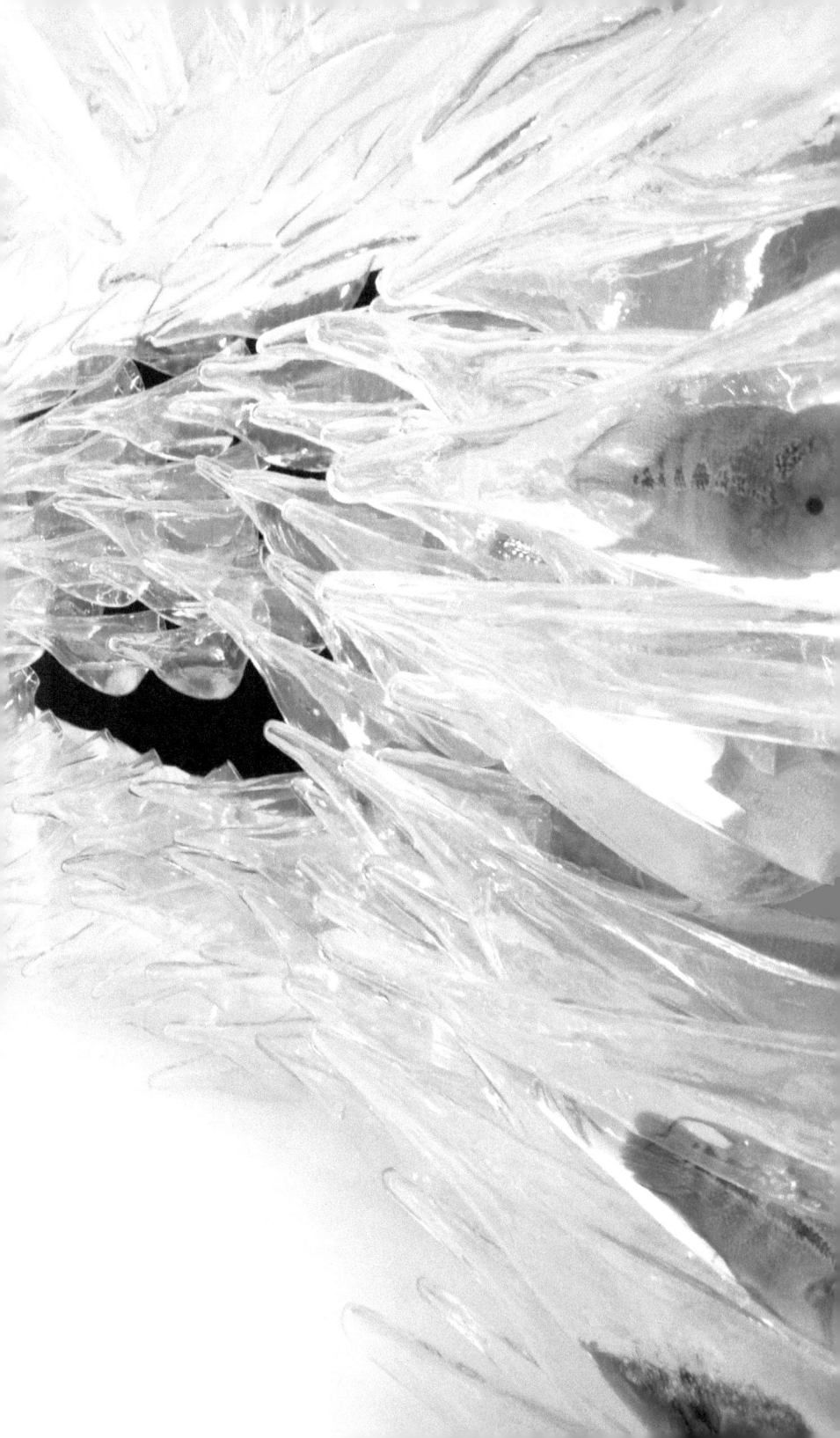

Credits
(by project)

(beau)strosity:

with RMIT University; TA/ Gwyllim Jahn; Director/ Anastasiya Vitusevych; Writer(s)/ Dan Schulz, Eleanor Tullock; Lead Cast/ Ad, Chanja; Supporting Cast/ Crystal Song Choo Jing, Dan Schulz, Vivian Kon Ching Sian; Cinematography/ Lila Athanasiadou; Set Director(s)/ Ada Umgofia, Crystal Song Choo Jing, Dan Schulz, Eleanor Tullock, Loo Yew Hann, Sam Verschoren, Vivian Kon Ching Sian; Sound Director/ Loo Yew Hann; Casting Director/ Tree; Security/ Crystal Song Choo Jing; Blood effect/ Eleanor Tullock; Editing/ Eleanor Tullock, Dan Schulz

concrete[i]land:

with Vongsawat Wongkijjalerd, Daniela Mitterberger; Michigan Architecture Students/ Po-Jen Huang, Te-Shiou Chen, Jakkrit Jannakhon, Linnea Cook, Salam Rida, Min Zhang, Weiqi Zhang, Stefan Klecheski, Beth Carliner, Peter Sepassi, Tracey Weisman, John Yoon

… Would Have Been My Last Complaint:

with/ Design Process & Computation/ Ezio Blasetti; Robotic Design/ Special effects, Stephan Henrich; Sound design/ Myrtille Fakhreddine(braïbraï), Devin Jernigan; Computation & Fabrication/ Mark-Henry Jean Decrausaz, Cameron David Newnham, Mark Kowalyov, Peeraya Suphasidh; Camera/ Suthiwat Yanawiboot; Storyboard/ Pim Jular; Model & Props/ Pajareeya Suriwong, Nichapatara Swangdecharux; Machinism Special Design/ Cheng Yu Ling; Shooting Organisation/ Wachira Leangtanom; Editing/ Camille Lacadee; Making-of/Danielle Willems, Pantira Unarat; Historical Research Assistant/ Natreeya Kraichitti; Community Negotiation Assistant/ Lila Tedesco; Production Assistants/ Arisa Juengsophonvitavas, Papat Jinaphun, Javed Godkin Paul de Costa, Nicha Laptaveepanya, Nuthapong Jiratiticharoen, Benjawan Lamsa-ard, Tachapol Danaboonchai, Suthata Jiranuntarat, Yanisa Chumpolphaisal, Jenwit Narukatphichai, Permpoon Rojanasakul; Construction/ Manjunath&Co; Engineer/ Ravi N.Pattegar, Civil Engineer Contractor; Acknowledgements/ Sri Ganapati Vedeshwar (Study Circle Library), Elias Tabet (Pandrata Circle), Sanjeen SingPawat, Gwyllim Jahn

La Passe:

with Andre Burger and Nicolas Ferron of Modern Pool Alpes; Draft/ Katrin Hochschuh, Hadin Charbel; Clients/ Daniele & Philippe Lacadee

the Offspring:

with Danielle Willems, Ezio Blasetti, Stephan Heinrich; Feral Child/ Syv Bruzeau; Siegmund & Sieglinde/ Chistopher Codam, Josefine Kallehave; Scenario Writing/ Ian Donaldson; Scenario Storyboard/Yujia Claire Bian; On-Set Props/ Johnny Bocquet-Boone; On-Set Hair & Makeup/ Dilsad Anil; Computation/ Dennis Schiaroli, Annie Locke-Scherer, Phil MarcAntonio, Yagiz Soylev; Construction Bamboo Structure/ Dennis Schiaroli, Phil

MarcAntonio, Annie Locke-Scherer, Ian Donaldson; Interior Components/
Ehsan Fazli, Alexandra Singer-Bieder, Agathe Michel; Props/ Shan
(Timothy) Sunderland, Johnny Bocquet-Boone, Ehsan Fazli, Dilsad Anil,
Yagiz Soylev; Editing/ Camille Lacadee; Sound/ Agatha Partyka; Special
Thanks to/ Vongsawat Wongkijjalerd, River Kwai Jungle Rafts Mon Village
& Sam Season

altered state:
with Carsten Höller; Computation/ Katrin Hochschuh; Installation/ CHD
construction Christian Huber Delisle; Curator/ Gabrielle Cram for Donau
Electronic Music Festival

Feral child (prelude):
with Jeremy Djaffer, Tiziano Derme; Performance/ Syv Bruzeau; Camera/
François Roche; Editing/ Camille Lacadee

∑ d a y s:
with RMIT University/ Gwyllim Jahn; Cast/ Natalie; Scenario/ Agatha
Partyka, Lynda Nguyen, Mark Kowalyov; Editing/ Agatha Partyka, Lynda
Nguyen; Direction/ Mark Kowalyov; Cinematography/ Grant Trewella;
Sound/ Agatha Partyka; Sound Recording/ Daniel Balacich; Morphology
Design/ Jack Mansfield-Hung, Victor Wong; Morphology Construction/ Zaid
Audi B Mohd Khorie, Victor Wong, Jack Mansfield-Hung; Rat Cage Design/
Christopher Ferris, Victor Wong; Translator - Local Liason/ Khunakorn
Terdkiatkhachorn; Fabrication/ Zaid Audi B Mohd Khorie, Khunakorn
Terdkiatkhachorn, Jack Mansfield-Hung; Fabrication Assistants/ Victor
Wong, Christopher Ferris, Mark Kowalyov, Daniel Balacich, Grant Trewella,
Agatha Partyka, Lynda Nguyen; Lighting/ Victor Wong, Zaid Audi B Mohd
Khorie; Costume & Make-up/ Lynda Nguyen; Props/ Jack Mansfield- Hung,
Lynda Nguyen; Supporting Cast/ Christopher Ferris, Jack Mansfield-Hung,
Lynda Nguyon, Zaid Audi B Mohd Khorie, Khunakorn Terdkiatkhachorn

WHATEVS~4~EVS:
with Vongsawat Wongkijjalerd, Amaury Thomas; Cast/ Nui; Hair & Make-
up/ Suwannee Surachescomson, Taweesit Mannark; UPenn// Scenario/
Jacqueline Martinez, Walaid Sehwail, Rhea Gargullo, Peter Wildfeuer;
Film Direction/ Jacqueline Martinez; Cinematography/ Walaid Sehwail;
Sound/ Rhea Gargullo; Lighting/ Peter Wildfeuer; Scenario & Script
Development/ Jacqueline Martinez, Peter Wildfeuer; Art Direction &
Props/ Rhea Gargullo, Walaid Sehwail; Production Assistants/ Billy
Wang, Michael Royer, Hyeji Yang, Geongu Lee; Grotto Design/ Michael
Royer; Grotto Fabrication/ Billy Wang, Michael Royer, Hyeji Yang,
Geongu Lee; Grotto Installation/ Billy Wang, Michael Royer, Hyeji Yang,
Geongu Lee, Jacqueline Martinez, Walaid Sehwail, Rhea Gargullo, Peter
Wildfeuer; Editing/ Camille Lacadee

| what could happen |:
with Pierre Huyghe (Mc Guffin), Daniela Mitterberger, Vongsawat
Wongkijjalerd; Curating/ Giorgio Pace Projects with Anne Ulrich;
Support/ LUMA Foundation, Louis Vuitton, Jurek and Ania Starak, Cabana,
Gaia Art Foundation, Canton Graubunden; Cast/ Veronique Mermoud,
Matthieu Kobilinski, Camille Lacadee; Camera/ François Roche; Editing/
Camille Lacadee, Daniela Mitterberger; Train Featuring/ Rick Owens &
Michèle Lamy; Installation/ CHD construction Christian Huber Delisle,
Edouard Lecuyer, Julien Borrel, Gauthier Martins; Mountain Guides/ Gian
Luck, Paul Rostetter; Train Management/ Jolanda Picenoni

Naxos (terra insōla):
with Danielle Willems, Lydia Kallipoliti, Ezio Blasetti, Stephan
Henrich, Andreas Theodoris, Luis Felipe Paris, Johnny Boquet-
Boone, Cecil Barnes, Danielle Griffo, Hasti Valipour Goudarzi, Gary
Edwards, Martin Lodman, Maximiliam Lauter, Melodie Yashar, Shalini
Amin, Pierre Bourdareau, George Avramides, George Louras, Jonathan
Requillo, Raquel Sanchis Ulacia, Robinson Strong, Kim Se Hyun, Lorenzo
Villaggi, Leonidas Leonidou; Partners/ Columbia University [GSAPP,
Graduate School of Architecture, Planning and Preservation], ΣΑΔΑΣ ΠΕΑ-
Τμήμα Χανίων, 'Ενωση Ξενοδόχων Νομού Χανίων, Οικονομικό Επιμελητήριο
Ελλάδος-Τμήμα Δυτικής Κρήτης, Περιφέρεια Κρήτης- Περιφερειακή Ενότητα
Χανίων, Πνευματικό Κέντρο Χανίων, 28η Εφορεία Βυζαντινών Αρχαιοτήτων,
Περιφερειακό Ταμείο Ανάπτυξης Κρήτης Sponsors/ ANEK Lines, INKA,
ΕΤΑΝΑΠ, ΒΙΟΧΥΜ ΑΕ, Αμπελώνες ΚΑΡΑΒΙΤΑΚΗ, Special Thanks to Roula, Soula
and Yorgos

Timidity Symptom:
with Cyril Lami, Jeep P. Narongthanarath; Collaborators/ Devin Jernigan,
Tiziano Derme, Myrtille Fakhreddine, Vongsawat Wongkijjalerd, Ip
Panit, Patrick Mc Kechnie, Katrin Hochschuh, Hadin Charbel…, Biennale
Installation/ Nicolas Grawitz and Iris Godbille, with Design Partners/
Ezio Blasetti (Mathematical Process), Andrew Snalune (Façade
Engineering), Sakkarn Sirisrisak (Steel Engineering), Sanitas Studio
(Landscape Architect); Movie// Performance/ Camille Lacadee; Make-up/
Taweesit Mannark; Production Assistant/ Iris Godbille; Client/ Petch
Osathanugrah

emet:
with RMIT University; TA/ Gwyllim Jahn; Cast/ Man trapped within
structure: Mr. Sankyu; Golem - Danica Yee; Kid 1: Chanchai, Kid 2:
Naowarat, Kid 3: Somsak, Story Writers/ Jordan Wells, James Pazzi,
Judy Junyan QI; Storyboarding/ Louis Nuccitelli; Directors/ Danica Yee,
Louis Nuccitelli; Cinematography/ Lucian Clifforth; Pre-editing/ Xiyue
Wang, Judy Junyan QI; Sound Designer/ Xiyue Wang; Lighting/ Jordan
Wells, James Pazzi; Set Designers/ Marc Gibson, James Pazzi; Fabrication
Team/ Marc Gibson, James Pazzi, Jordan Wells, Dechao Sun, Bowen Nie,

Zhen Tian, Judy Junyan QI; Props/ Louis Nuccitelli, Lucian Clifforth, Danica Yee, Xiyue Wang; Make up + Costume Designers/ Judy Junyan Qi, Marc Gibson, Jordan Wells; Thai-Translator & Local Liaison/ Dechao Sun; Robotics/ Vongsawat Wongkijjalerd; Editing/ Camille Lacadee, Daniela Mitterberger

Daemon in BKK:
with Nutthapong Jiratthiticharoen, Natreeya Kraichitti, Thanaporn Lam, Pisut Phumchaosoun, Jariyaporn Prachasartta, Sitthiwat Suddhijaru, Bahnfun Chittmittrapap; Choregraphy/ Jitti Chompee; Photography/ Basil Childers

Zeitgast:
with University of Innsbruck (institute for experimental architecture.hochbau); Robot/ Stephan Henrich; Assistant Producer/ Galo Moncayo Asan, Marc Ihle, Peter Griebel; Cast/ Martina Lesjak; Scenario/ Alexander Grasser, Jörg Stanzel; Props/ Lukas Härtenberger, Philipp Rust, Theresa Uitz; Robotic Suit/ Lino Lanzmaier, Pedja Gavrilovic, Simeon Brugger; Cinematography/ Alexander Nikolas Walzer, Gülay Güldemir; Theresa Uitz; Sound Recording/ Alexander Nikolas Walzer, Gülay Güldemir; Make-up/ Gülay Güldemir; Camera/ François Roche; Editing/ Camille Lacadee; Support/ Spielraum - Fablab Innsbruck, Rexlab, Institute For Archeology - University of Innsbruck, Agrargemeinschaft Haggen; Sponsors, Partners/ institute for experimental architecture.hochbau, Vice Rector for Research, Dean of The Faculty of Architecture

Although (in) hapnea:
with Katrin Hochschuh, FabLab Thammasat University Bangkok/ Samustpon Tanapant, Arisa Plapiriyakit, Nonsthorn Srisuphanraj, Trin Chanchaiprasong, Pongsakorn Sarunsatta, Supinda Bannapob, Nonglak Boonsang Nuttapol Techopitch, Tanakorn Somsuk, Piyanut Songkhroh; Co-Production/ Graham Foundation Chicago, Nouveau Musée National de Monaco, CNC DICREAM; Journalist and Ophelia/ Camille Lacadee; Creature/ Sarut Komalittipong; Interzone Fishermadman/ Khun Pan; Glass Blowing/ Union Victors Co, Ltd Bangkok; Sound Design and Mix/ Myrtille Fakhreddine; Guitar/ Nader Mekdachi; Make-up/ Suwannee Surachescomson, Taweesit Mannark; Cinematography/ Francois Roche; Editing/ Camille Lacadee; Ephemeral Direction Assistant/ Sompot Chidgasornpongse; Production Assistant/ Hadin Charbel; Special Thanks to/ Makkasan community in Bangkok, Sompong, Toon, Pai, Tree and Mr Sankyu

Index & neologisms

First published in 2015
by punctum books * brooklyn, new york
http://punctumbooks.com

punctum books is an independent, open-access publisher
dedicated to radically creative modes of intellectual inquiry
and writing across a whimsical para-humanities assemblage.
We solicit and pimp quixotic, sagely mad engagements with
textual thought-bodies, and provide shelters for intellectual
vagabonds.

ISBN-13: 978-0692523551
ISBN-10: 0692523553

Back Cover Text: Eileen A. Joy

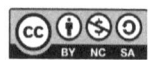

www.ingramcontent.com/pod-product-compliance
Lightning Source LLC
Chambersburg PA
CBHW040904180526
45159CB00010BA/2922